E SSENTIAL
G RAN CANARIA

★ Best places to see 34–55   ■ Featured sight

700035323349

Original text by Gabrielle MacPhedran
Updated by Sally Roy

© Automobile Association Developments Limited 2009
First published 2007
Reprinted 2009. Information verified and updated

ISBN: 978-0-7495-6010-2

Published by AA Publishing, a trading name of Automobile Association Developments
Limited, whose registered office is Fanum House, Basing View, Basingstoke,
Hampshire RG21 4EA. Registered number 1878835.

Colour separation: MRM Graphics Ltd
Printed and bound in Italy by Printer Trento S.r.l.

A03616
Maps in this title produced from mapping:
© KOMPASS GmbH, A-6063 Rum.Innsbruck

About this book

Symbols are used to denote the following categories:

➕ map reference to maps on cover

✉ address or location

☎ telephone number

🕐 opening times

✋ admission charge

🍴 restaurant or café on premises or nearby

Ⓜ nearest underground train station

🚌 nearest bus/tram route

🚊 nearest overground train station

⛴ nearest ferry stop

✈ nearest airport

ℹ tourist office information

❓ other practical information

▶ indicates the page where you will find a fuller description

This book is divided into five sections.

The essence of Gran Canaria
pages 6–19
Introduction; Features; Food and Drink;
Short Break including the 10 Essentials

Planning pages 20–33
Before You Go; Getting There; Getting
Around; Being There

Best places to see pages 34–55
The unmissable highlights of any visit
to Gran Canaria

Best places to go pages 56–77
Excellent restaurants; places to take
the children; activities; museums and
art galleries; places to be entertained
and more

Exploring pages 78–186
The best places to visit in Gran Canaria,
organized by area

Maps
All map references are to the maps on
the covers. For example, Teror has the
reference ➕ 8D – indicating the grid
square in which it is to be found.

Admission prices
Inexpensive (under €5)
Moderate (€5 –€8)
Expensive (over €8)

Hotel prices
Price are per room per night:
€ budget (under €90);
€€ moderate (€90–€150);
€€€ expensive to luxury (over €150).

Restaurant prices
Price for a three-course meal per person
without drinks:
€ budget (under €20);
€€ moderate (€20–€30);
€€€ expensive (over €30).

Contents

BEST THINGS TO DO

56 – 77

EXPLORING...

78 – 186

The essence of...

Golden sands and blue seas are the essence of Gran Canaria for most visitors, but there are increasing numbers of people who come here to windsurf, sail, fish, play golf, mountain-bike, fly planes or paraglide. Walkers and botanists find the island irresistible. As for nightlife, there is enough choice of clubs, cabarets, pubs, discos and casinos to satisfy any taste, mainstream or alternative, and at any decibel level. But whichever way you choose to enjoy the island, those seas and sands are never far away.

features

Most people come to Gran Canaria for its abundant sunshine and its golden beaches. They head for the south and the guaranteed rain-free resorts such as Playa del Inglés, Maspalomas and Puerto Rico. Here, the pleasures of sun and rest and recreation often prove so seductive that some never set foot outside their resort except to catch the plane back home. So they miss the one essential characteristic of Gran Canaria – its diversity.

Consider the geography: to the west, the island rises to cliffs of jagged black rock, pounded by a spume-laced sea. Among the northern hills, clouds can blot out the sun for hours at a time – an astonishment to southern residents. Equally unexpected to some is the central range of volcanic peaks, the highest of which can attract snow in winter. From these rocky heights, forests of pine trees descend to hillsides spiky with euphorbia and prickly pear. The central valleys are lush and green, some of them extraordinarily fertile, with palms sprouting like feather dusters among mangoes, pineapple and papaya.

There is majestic landscape and rural tranquillity in abundance. But do not ignore the capital, Las Palmas, or the smaller towns. After decades of neglect by central government, greater local autonomy and European funds have resulted in a striking face-lift of the island and a growing self-confidence among its people.

GEOGRAPHY

● Situated in the Atlantic Ocean, 210km (130 miles) from the African coastline and 1,250km (775 miles) from Cádiz, Gran Canaria is the third largest of the seven major islands of the Canarian archipelago. The largest are Tenerife and Fuerteventura, though Gran Canaria has the greatest population.

● It is a circular, volcanic island which last erupted seriously about 3,000 years ago. It has an area of 1,532sq km (598sq miles) and the land comes down steeply from the high central peaks, with vast *barrancos* – dry water courses or ravines – running to the coast like the spokes of a bicycle wheel.

CAPITAL

● Gran Canaria's capital city, Las Palmas, is also capital of the province bearing the same name. This consists of Gran Canaria and the other eastern islands, Fuerteventura and Lanzarote. The western islands, including Tenerife, La Palma, Gomera and El Hierro, form the province of Tenerife. Together, since 1983, the two provinces have made up the Autonomous Region of the Canary Islands.

POPULATION

● Gran Canaria has a population of 790,000 with 380,000 of them living in Las Palmas.

FACTS AND FIGURES

● The number of annual visitors is 2,820,000.
● The highest point is Pico (Pozo de las Nieves (1,949m/6,393ft).

food & drink

Spaniards love eating out, and Canarians are no exception. Given the number of visitors here, it is no surprise that the island offers every kind of Spanish and European food. But Canarian food is rather different: country cooking, revealing a deep love for the island's own ingredients.

MAIN DISHES

Top of the list and found everywhere are *papas arrugadas* ('wrinkly potatoes'). These are small potatoes, boiled in their skins in water and coarse salt: 'saltier than the sea', says one local recipe book. They are eaten with a sauce called *mojo*. *Mojo verde*, or green *mojo*, is made with oil and vinegar, garlic, cumin, coriander (cilantro) and parsley; in *mojo rojo*, or red *mojo*, paprika is substituted for the coriander and parsley; and there is *mojo picon*, with a bracing dose of chilli. Taste before you dollop, especially the red varieties. These sauces are also served with fish and meat.

Less obvious to the visitor, since it is not often served in restaurants, is a form of cereal called *gofio*, which is traditional Canarian comfort food. This has been the staple diet for hundreds of years and it has survived almost unchanged to this day. Essentially this is any cereal – typically wheat or maize – toasted, then milled, and served either as a breakfast-type cereal with milk; moistened and made into little balls

(a dumpling substitute); as a thickening in stews and soups, or as an addition to almost any kind of drink. This is the essential food of home and hearth.

Other rustic dishes on the Gran Canarian menu include rabbit, usually served in stews, and hearty *sancocho*, a great favourite in bars and simple eateries. *Sancocho* consists of salt fish, usually in chunks, soaked and boiled, and served with *papas arrugadas*, *mojo* sauce and balls of *gofio*.

Among the Atlantic fish that are caught in the waters off Gran Canaria are *cherne* (a kind of grouper), *sama*

(bream) and *vieja* (parrotfish). The most common is *cherne*, which is generally casseroled or poached with potatoes and coriander. In fishing ports such as Arguineguín and Puerto de Mogán, there's always *pescado fresco* (fresh fish) on the menu. This deliberately vague term allows the restaurant to serve whatever the local fishermen have brought in, which will be simply grilled with garlic and herbs and is invariably delicious.

In the Canary Islands, *queso* (cheese) is generally eaten as a starter rather than after the meal. The main varieties are *queso tierno* (a soft goat's cheese), *queso curado* (mature sheep's or goat's cheese, such as Majorero from Fuerteventura) and *queso de flor*, produced in the highlands of Guía and curdled with thistle flowers.

ISLAND DRINKS

On an island where fruit is mostly tropical and subtropical – mangoes and papaya are common – the local fruit juice is well worth tasting; and Gran Canaria also produces its own excellent mineral waters.

Of other drinks, wine is produced in small quantities, especially in the Bandamas area, around Santa Brígida. A number of *bodegas* can be found in and around Monte de Lentiscal, and quality is said to be improving. In San Bartolomé de Tirajana a local liqueur called *guindilla* is made from the *guinda* (sour cherry). A lemon-flavoured liqueur called *mejunje* is made in Santa Lucía. More popular across the island is local rum, *Arehucas*, made in Arucas on a base of sugar cane. Canarian workers are inclined to take a shot of it at breakfast time.

CANARIAN DESSERTS

On Gran Canaria desserts are not a culinary adventure. Apart from *flan*, a custard pudding popular throughout Spain, the local speciality is *bienmesabe* ('how good it tastes'). Made from almonds and honey, it is often used as a sauce poured over ice-cream. Nougat and marzipan are other local products.

CANARIAN SPECIALITIES

● *conejo en salmorejo* – rabbit marinated in garlic, parsley, oregano, thyme and vinegar, then basted in wine and served in an earthenware dish with *papas arrugadas*.

● *gofio escaldado* – gofio stirred into fish stock to produce a thick paste.

● *papas arrugadas* (➤ 12).

● *potaje de berros* – watercress soup, which may also include potatoes, sweet potatoes and bacon.

● *puchero canario* – a hearty meat and vegetable casserole that typically contains beef, pork, chicken, sausage, chickpeas, marrow, sweetcorn, carrots, beans, tomatoes, onion and pears, served with *gofio* dumplings to soak up the stock.

● *rancho canario* – a stew of meat, potatoes, chickpeas, tomatoes and noodles.

● *ropa vieja* – literally 'old clothes', this consists of chickpeas fried with diced meat and vegetables and was created as a way to use up leftovers.

● *sancocho* – the most typical Canarian dish of all, this is salt fish and potato stew, served with *papas arrugadas*, *gofio* and *mojo* sauce.

short break

If you have only a short time to visit Gran Canaria and would like to take home some unforgettable memories you can do something local and capture the real flavour of the island. The following suggestions will give you a wide range of sights and experiences that won't take very long, won't cost much and will make your visit very special. If you only have time to choose just one of these, you will have found the true heart of Gran Canaria.

● **Watch the sunset** over the sea from the lighthouse at Maspalomas (➤ 112–113). Anglers cast their lines from the rocks, shadows deepen among the dunes, children trail home across wide sands after a sundrenched day.

● **Take a boat trip** from Arguineguín (➤ 105) or Puerto Rico (➤ 126–127) to Puerto de Mogán (➤ 50–51), last resort village on the west coast, for a view of the island from the sea.

● **Linger in the sun** at a terrace café in the Parque Santa Catalina (➤ 87), in Las Palmas. Watch the locals play chess and dominoes at outdoor tables.

● **Walk in the Tamadaba pine forest** (► 154) with soft pine needles underfoot and undergrowth of cistus and thyme. Look down to the harbour at Puerto de las Nieves (► 170), far below, and across the sea to Mount Teide on Tenerife.

● **Make a weekend visit** to the Jardín Botánico Canario in Tafira (► 46–47). Bridal parties come in droves to be photographed in this verdant setting.

● **Visit the ancient religious site** of the island's aboriginal people at Cuatro Puertas (► 167). Look from the top of the windswept hill to imagine a time before the Spaniards arrived.

- **Have a coffee** in the lounge of the Santa Catalina hotel (➤ 95) in Las Palmas. All celebrity visitors to the island stay here, including the Spanish monarch, King Juan Carlos.

- **See a Canarian wrestling match,** or *lucha canaria*, a team sport dating from pre-Spanish, Guanche times which sends the usually restrained Canarios wild with excitement.

- **Drive eastwards from Pasito Blanco** (➤ 119) on the old coast road at night for an unexpected view of the lights of Maspalomas and Playa del Inglés, like a shimmering blanket of stars.

- **Catch a performance** of Canarian folk singing and dancing in Las Palmas at the Pueblo Canario (➤ 75) on Sunday morning.

Planning

Before you go

WHEN TO GO

JAN	FEB	MAR	APR	MAY	JUN	JUL	AUG	SEP	OCT	NOV	DEC
19°C	19°C	19°C	20°C	21°C	21°C	23°C	24°C	24°C	25°C	25°C	19°C
66°F	66°F	66°F	68°F	70°F	70°F	73°F	75°F	75°F	77°F	77°F	66°F

● High season ● Low season

The temperatures above are the average daily maximum for each month. Minimum temperatures rarely drop below 15°C (59°F); there is a year-round spring climate. On the south coast, which has over 300 days of sun a year, summer temperatures often exceed 30°C (80°F). The sea temperature varies from 19°C (66°F) in January to 24°C (75°F) in September. Most of the rain falls in the north, and there is occasional snow in the central mountains. The north is also affected by the *mar de nubes* (sea of clouds), low-lying clouds brought by the trade winds, and the *panza de burro* (donkey's belly), a grey haze producing intense heat in summer. The summer, particularly in July and August, is when many Spanish families are on holiday.

WHAT YOU NEED

● Required
○ Suggested
▲ Not required

Some countries require a passport to remain valid for a minimum period (usually at least six months) beyond the date of entry – contact the consulate or embassy or your travel agent for details.

	UK	Germany	USA	Netherlands	Spain
Passport (or National Identity Card where applicable)	●	●	●	●	▲
Visa (regulations can change – check before you travel)	▲	▲	▲	▲	▲
Onward or Return Ticket	▲	▲	●	▲	▲
Health Inoculations (tetanus and polio)	▲	▲	▲	▲	▲
Health Documentation (► 23, Health Advice)	●	●	●	●	▲
Travel Insurance	○	○	○	○	○
Driving Licence (national)	●	●	●	●	●
Car Insurance Certificate	●	●	●	●	●
Car Registration Document	●	●	●	●	●

WEBSITES

Spanish Tourist Board:
www.tourspain.es
www.tourspain.co.uk
www.spain.info
www.okspain.org

Gran Canaria Tourist Board:
www.grancanaria.com

Maspalomas Costa Canaria:
www.maspalomas.com

TOURIST OFFICES AT HOME

In the UK SpanishTourist Office
✉ 22–23 Manchester Square,
London WIU 3PX
☎ 0207 486 8077

In the USA Tourist Office of Spain
✉ 666 Fifth Avenue 35th Floor

New York, NY 10103
☎ 212/265-8822

Tourist Office of Spain
✉ 8383 Wilshire Boulevard, Suite
960, Beverly Hills, CA 90211
☎ 323/658-7188

HEALTH ADVICE

Insurance Nationals of EU and certain other countries receive free
medical treatment in the Canaries with the relevant documentation (EHIC
– European Health Insurance Card). Private medical insurance is still
advised and essential for other visitors.

Dental services Dental treatment has to be paid for by all visitors. There
are many English-speaking dentists; your hotel or tourist information
centre will inform you of the nearest one. Private medical insurance will
cover emergency dental costs.

TIME DIFFERENCES

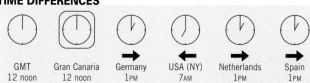

GMT	Gran Canaria	Germany	USA (NY)	Netherlands	Spain
12 noon	12 noon	1PM	7AM	1PM	1PM

Gran Canaria, like the rest of the Canaries, is in the same time zone as the
UK, which is 1 hour behind most of Europe. The islands change to
Summer Time (GMT +1) on the same date as the UK and the rest of the
EU. The Canaries are 1 hour behind mainland Spain.

PLANNING

NATIONAL HOLIDAYS

1 January *New Year's Day*
6 January *Epiphany*
19 March *St Joseph's Day*
March/April
*Maundy Thursday, Good
Friday and Easter Monday*
1 May *Labour Day*
30 May *Canary Island Day*
May/June *Corpus Cristi*

15 August *Assumption of
the Virgin*
8 September
Birthday of the Virgin Mary
12 October *National Day*
1 November *All Saints'
Day*
6 December
Constitution Day

8 December
*Feast of the Immaculate
Conception*
25 December
Christmas Day
*Most shops, offices and
museums close on these
days.*

WHAT'S ON WHEN

January *Festival of the Three Kings* (6 January): gifts for the children.

February *Almond Blossom Festival*, Tejeda and Valsequillo: song and dance.
Carnival: street bands and parties, with some of the most spectacular parades in Europe.

March Arguineguín celebrates the feast day of Santa Agueda.

March/April *Semana Santa* (Holy Week): celebrated throughout the island.

Late May/early June *Feast of Corpus Cristi:* streets are decorated with flowers and sand.
San Juan festival: Anniversary of the foundation of Las Palmas, when cultural events take place in the city.

July *Fiestas del Carmen* (16 July): celebrated by all fishing villages.
Feast day of Santiago (25 July): in Gáldar and San Bartolomé – Gáldar has wrestling, picnics and dancing.

August *Bajada de la Rama* (4 August): celebrated in Agaete, this is probably the most popular festival on the island. It originates from an ancient aboriginal rite of praying for rain. Local people climbed high into the pine forests and brought down branches to thrash the sea. Modern Canarios do the same. This is a great opportunity to get wet and have a party.

September *Fiesta de La Virgen del Pino* (Our Lady of the Pine, 8 September): held in Teror, pilgrims come from all over Gran Canaria in celebration of the island's patron saint, many of them walking through the night to Teror. They bring cartfuls of produce, which are placed before the image of the Virgin in the square and then dispensed to poor folk later. *Fiesta del Charco* (10 September): in San Nicolás de Tolentino.

October *Fiestas de Nuestra Señora del Rosario* (Our Lady of the Rosary, 5 October): celebrated in Agüimes, with Canarian stick-fighting and wrestling.
La Naval (6 October): held in Las Palmas, this commemorates the successful repulsion of the English privateer Francis Drake in 1595.
Fiesta de la Manza (first Sunday in October): celebrates the apple harvest

with a festival in Valleseco, near Teror.

November *Festival of San Martín de Porres* (first week in November): Arinaga.

December *Fiesta de los Labradores* (20 December): people celebrate by dressing in peasant costume and carrying old-fashioned farming tools in Santa Lucía.

Getting there

BY AIR

Gando Airport

22km (14 miles) to city centre

N/A

20 minutes

20 minutes

Most visitors arrive on charter flights direct from western Europe. There are numerous charter flights to Las Palmas throughout the year from London and other European cities. Most seats are sold by tour operators as part of a package holiday, but it is also possible to buy a flight only through travel agents or on the internet. For independent travellers, the disadvantage of charter flights is that you are usually restricted to periods of seven or fourteen days.

Budget airlines, such as easyJet (www.easyjet.co.uk) and Ryanair (www.ryanair.co.uk), offer an increasing number of direct flights to Gran Canaria from various UK airports, allowing far more flexibility. Check their websites for further details.

Monarch Airlines (www.flymonarch.com) also operate frequent inexpensive scheduled flights direct to Gran Canaria from London. From the USA, Canada, Australia and New Zealand, it is often cheaper to fly to London or Amsterdam and pick up a charter flight from there. Flight times are about four hours from London and two hours from Madrid.

It's 22km (14 miles) from Gando Airport (the offical name of the airport) to Las Palmas and takes 15 to 20 minutes, depending on the type of public transport used.

BY SEA

The ferry company Trasmediterránea (tel: 902 45 46 45 on Gran Canaria; www.trasmediterranea.co.uk) has a weekly car ferry service from Cádiz on the Spanish mainland to Tenerife and Gran Canaria. The journey from Cádiz to Las Palmas takes around 38 hours. The Puerto de la Luz ferry terminal is 3km (2 miles) from Las Palmas and the journey takes from 5 to 10 minutes, depending on the traffic conditions.

CUSTOMS

As the Canaries are a free-trade zone there are no limits on the amounts of alcohol, tobacco, perfume and other goods (except for gifts of value greater than €48) that can be brought into the islands. Visitors may bring an unlimited amount of foreign currency in to the Canaries but should declare any amount exceeding the equivalent of €6,000 to avoid difficulties on leaving.

Drugs, firearms, ammunition, offensive weapons, obscene material and unlicensed animals are not permitted.

Getting around

PUBLIC TRANSPORT

Buses Global Salcai Utinsa is the main operator (tel: 902 38 11 10; www.globalsu.net). Services, including express, run from Las Palmas to resorts in the south and to many towns and villages in the centre and the north. Services are reasonably frequent and start from the bus station at Parque San Telmo (tel: 928 36 83 35). Always check bus numbers used in this guide before making your journey.

Urban transport In Las Palmas, the Guaguas Municipales (city bus service) runs three routes (1, 2, 3) leaving from Bus Station Square, the Plaza de Cairasco or General Franco, depending on their destination. City suburb services start from the Plaza del Mercado. Smaller towns such as Telde, Santa Lucía, Arucas, Santa María de Guía and Gáldar have their own buses. An open-deck, hop-on-hop-off tourist bus, the Guagua Turística, operates in Las Palmas, covering the entire city and its sights.

INTER-ISLAND FLIGHTS

All of the main Canary Islands have an airport and are interconnected by air. The main operators are Binter Canarias (tel: 902 39 13 92; www.binternet.com), Iberia (tel: 902 40 05 00; www.iberia.com) and Air Europa (tel: 928 57 95 84; www.air-europa.com).

Flight times are around 30 minutes. Flights between Gran Canaria and Tenerife are almost hourly. Inter-island flights are well used by islanders and early booking is essential.

INTER-ISLAND FERRIES

All of the Canary Islands can be reached by ferry, most of these run by Irasmediterránea (tel: 902 45 46 45 www.trasmediterranea.es), departing daily from Puerto de la Luz just outside Las Palmas.

There is also a regular jetfoil/hydrofoil service ARMAS (tel: 902 45 65 00, 928 26 77 00; www.naviera-armas.com) between Las Palmas (Gran Canaria) and Santa Cruz (Tenerife) – 100 minutes – and Morro Jable (Fuerteventura).

Fred Olsen (tel: 902 10 01 07; 928 49 50 40; www.fredolsen.es) runs eight ferries a day from Puerto de Las Nieves (Agaete) to Santa Cruz in Tenerife, with a journey time of one hour.

FARES AND CONCESSIONS

If you are staying in the south you can buy a book of 10 bus tickets for travel between the resorts (€8); these are available from the main bus station in Playa del Inglés. In Las Palmas the Guagua Turistica ticket is valid all day; buy it on board or in Santa Catalina, San Telmo or next to the Teatro Pérez. For further information tel: 928 30 58 00 or check out www.guaguas.com.

Tourist attractions in the south will often offer a combined family ticket for two adults and two children; ask at the tourist office (➤ 30).

TAXIS

Taxis are identified by the letters SP *(servicio público)* on the front and rear bumpers. Most are metered at a rate fixed by the municipal authorities. For short trips in tourist areas the meter will normally be switched off. There are usually fixed rates for long distances. If you are unsure, check before you start your journey.

DRIVING

- Drive on the right. Seat belts must be worn in front seats at all times and in rear seats where fitted.

  Speed limits on *autopistas* and *autovias:* 120kph (75mph).

  Speed limits on country roads: 90kph (56mph).

  Speed limits on urban roads: 50kph (31mph).

  Speed limits in residential areas: 20kph (12mph).

- An international driving licence is required for North American visitors.
- There is random breath-testing. Never drive under the influence of alcohol.
- Petrol stations should be easy to find along main roads with 24-hour opening in the larger resorts and towns, though some only open until 2pm on Sunday.
- If you break down in your own car the Royal Automobile Club of Gran Canaria, Léon y Castillo 279 (tel: 928 23 07 88), can offer advice on breakdown and repair services. Repairs are usually dealt with promptly. If the car is hired, telephone the local office of the firm and be sure to follow the instructions given in your rental documentation.

CAR RENTAL

There are plenty of car rental firms, usually offering unlimited mileage. Prices vary considerably between large rental companies and small local firms; shop around, keeping in mind that rates may either be genuinely competitive or reflect hazardous corner-cutting in maintenance.

Being there

TOURIST OFFICES

Patronato de Turismo Gran Canaria (Local Tourist Authority)
León y Castillo 17
35003 Las Palmas de Gran Canaria
☎ 928 21 96 01
www.grancanaria.com

Oficina de Turismo Las Palmas
Las Palmas de Gran Canaria
☎ 928 44 68 24

Centro Insular de Turismo (Tourism Insular Centre) Centro
Commercial Yumbo
Playa del Inglés
☎ 928 77 15 50

Avenida de Mogán Puerto
Puerto Rico
☎ 928 56 00 29
www.turismo.mogan.es

Oficina Municipal de Turismo de Agüimes
Plaza de San Anton 1
☎ 928 12 41 83

Most towns and some larger villages have a local tourist office. Opening times vary and most close for the weekend.

MONEY

Currency The unit of currency is the euro (€). Coins are issued in denominations of 1, 2, 5, 10, 20 and 50 euro cents and €1 and €2. There are 100 cents in €1. Notes (bills) are issued in denominations of €5, €10, €20, €50, €100, €200 and €500.

Exchange You can exchange travellers' cheques at some banks and at bureaux de change at airports, main railway stations or in some department stores, and exchange booths. All transactions are subject to a

TIPS/GRATUITIES

Yes ✓ No ✗		
Restaurants (if service not included)	✓	10%
Cafés/bars	✓	loose change
Taxis	✓	10%
Porters	✓	€1–€2/bag
Chambermaids	✓	€1–€2/week
Toilets	✗	

hefty commission charge, so you may prefer to rely on cash and credit cards. Travellers' cheques issued by American Express and VISA can also be changed at many post offices.

Credit cards are widely accepted in shops, restaurants and hotels. VISA, MasterCard and Diners Club cards with four-digit PINs can be used in most ATM cash dispensers.

POSTAL AND INTERNET SERVICES

Post boxes are yellow. Use the slot marked *extranjero* (foreign) for sending postcards home. Post offices *(correos)* sell stamps *(sellos* or *timbres)* and provide telegram and fax services (Mon–Fri 8:30–8:30, Sat 9:30–2).

You'll find internet points in many of the larger hotels, for which a small fee is charged, or you can log on at one of the internet cafés found in all the resorts.

TELEPHONES

Light-blue public telephone booths *(cabina de teléfono)* are the most economical option. Most take coins, credit cards or a phonecard *(credifone)*, available from post offices and some shops. Or use a *telefónica* cabin where the phone is metered and you pay after your call.

Emergency telephone numbers

Police 112 or 092 (Local Police) or 091 (State Police)
Fire 112 or 080 (Las Palmas)

Ambulance 112 or 061
Hospital 928 45 00 00 (Las Palmas)

EMBASSIES AND CONSULATES

UK: ☎ 928 26 25 08
Germany: ☎ 928 49 18 80

USA: ☎ 928 22 25 52
Netherlands: ☎ 928 36 22 51

HEALTH AND SAFETY

Sun advice The south of the island has virtual year-round sunshine, which is at its strongest in summer. The north of the island is often cooler but you should wear sun-screen whatever the time of year.

Pharmacies Prescription and non-prescription medicines are available from *farmacias* (pharmacies), distinguished by a large green cross. They can dispense many drugs available only on prescription in other countries.

Safe water Tap water is generally safe but is not recommended for its taste. Anywhere, but especially outside tourist resorts, it is advisable to drink bottled water *(agua mineral)*, sold either *sin gaz* (still) or *con gaz* (carbonated).

Personal safety Violence against visitors is unusual. Theft from cars is the most common form of crime, particularly in Las Palmas. There are three police forces: Policía Municipal (blue uniforms), Policía Nacional (brown uniforms) and Guardia Civil (green uniforms). To help them and yourself, there are a number of precautions you can take:

● Do not leave valuables on the beach or poolside, or in your car.

● Leave valuables in hotel safe deposit boxes.

● Avoid the seamier streets of Las Palmas at night.

ELECTRICITY

The power supply is 220 volts in older buildings, but 110 volts in newer ones. Sockets take two-prong, round-pin plugs. Visitors from the UK require an adaptor and US visitors need a voltage transformer. Power cuts sometimes happen, so pack a torch.

OPENING HOURS

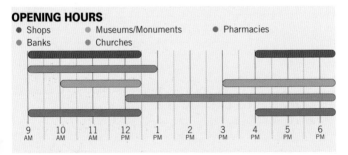

● Shops   ● Museums/Monuments   ● Pharmacies
● Banks   ● Churches

| 9 AM | 10 AM | 11 AM | 12 PM | 1 PM | 2 PM | 3 PM | 4 PM | 5 PM | 6 PM |

In addition to the times above, some shops in the busier resorts stay open until later in the evening and open on Sunday. Department stores are open 10 to 8. Some shops (including pharmacies) close on Saturday afternoons.

Bank winter opening times are 8–3 (Saturday until 1pm). Banks are closed Sunday all year. The opening times of museums is variable; some close Saturday afternoon and all day Sunday, others on Monday (or another weekday), while some remain open all week.

LANGUAGE

It is helpful to know some basic Spanish. Pronunciation guide: *b* almost like a *v*; *c* before *e* or *i* sounds like *th* otherwise like *k*; *d* like English *d* or *th*; *g* before *e* or *i* is a guttural *h*, between vowels like *h*, otherwise like *g*; *h* always silent; *j* guttural *h*; *ll* like English *lli* (as in 'million'); *ñ* sounds like *ni* in 'onion'; *qu* sound like *k*; *v* sounds a little like *b*; *z* like English *th*.

yes/no	*si/no*	I don't speak	*No hablo*
please/thank you	*por favor/gracias*	Spanish	*español*
hello/hi/good day	*hola/buenos dias*	I am .../I have ..	*Soy .../Tengo ...*
sorry, pardon me	*perdon*	help!	*socorro!*
bye, see you	*hasta luego*	how much	*cuánto es?*
that's fine	*está bien*	open/closed	*abierto/cerrado*
what?	*como?*	the toilet	*los servicios*

hotel	*hotel*	reservation	*una reserva*
room	*una habitación*	rate	*la tarifa*
single/double/ twin	*individual/doble/*	breakfast	*el desayuno*
	con dos camas	bathroom	*el cuarto de baño*
one/two nights	*una noche/dos*	shower	*la ducha*
	noches	key	*la llave*

bureau de change	*cambio*	fpounds sterling	*la libra esterlina*
post office	*correos*	banknote	*un billete de banco*
cash machine/ATM	*cajero automático*	travellers' cheques	*cheques de viaje*
foreign exchange	*cambio (de divisas)*	credit card	*tarjeta de crédito*

restaurant/cafe-bar	*restaurante/bar*	dessert	*el postre*
table/menu	*una mesa/la carta*	water/beer	*agua/cerveza*
today's set menu	*el plato del día*	(house) wine	*vino (de la casa)*
wine list	*la carta de vinos*	bill	*la cuenta*

plane	*el avion*	ticket	*un billete*
airport	*el aeropuerto*	single/return...	*de ida / ...de ida y*
bus	*el autobús*		*vuelta*
	('guagua')	timetable	*el horario*
ferry/terminal	*el ferry/terminus*	seat	*un asiento*

Best places to see

1 Andén Verde

Andén Verde, or 'Green Platform', is the name given to a magnificent stretch of corniche road on the northwest coast.

Winding northeast along the cliff-face, the road offers thrilling glimpses downwards, by way of plummeting rock, to a vertiginously distant sea. Though the extent of the Andén Verde is a little vague, this most exciting part of the west coast effectively begins a short way north of San Nicolás de Tolentino (➤ 129).

Running just inland for 6km (4 miles) or so from San Nicolás, the road suddenly veers towards a gap in a hill-crest above the sea. There is a small car park here, the Mirador del Balcón, or 'Balcony Lookout Point'. Though views from the car park are very fine, it is worth descending the few steps to a lower platform. From here, the rocks beneath, and the cliff foot to the southwest, may be seen clearly. The cliff is surmounted by a dramatic series of hills, each of them terminating suddenly in a triangle of dark cliff. Each successive triangle is a little lower than the one before, their diminishing height marking the descent towards the harbour at Puerto de la Aldea (➤ 124–125). The island of Tenerife lies west across the water.

The road continues to the northeast, following the cliff. There are one or two further spots where cars can pull off the road, sometimes with difficulty, so take care. As the Andén Verde draws to a close the road swings inland, descending towards the little village of El Risco.

✚ 2D ✉ Passes through the districts of Mogán (➤ 115), San Nicolás de Tolentino (➤ 129) and Agaete (➤ 160)
🍴 Fruit and fast-food van in the Mirador del Balcón car park (€) 🚌 101 San Nicolas Tolentino–Gáldar

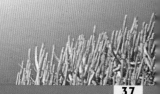

2 Barranco de Guayadeque

This is an enchanting canyon southwest of the airport, on the eastern side of the island, and a centre of population in pre-Spanish times.

Lying between the municipalities of Ingenio and Agüimes, this *barranco* is more praised by environmentalists than any other on the island. From the flat floor of the dry river bed, the walls of the ravine rise through green terraces of cultivation, through tall palms, silvery eucalyptus and the soft green ping-pong bats of prickly pear, to lofty crags of red volcanic rock.

Many of the island's rarest plants grow here, and much of the *barranco* has been designated a nature reserve. The 80 endemic species of flora found here include the *Kunkelliela canariensis* and *Helianthemum tholiforme*.

The aboriginal people who once lived in this fertile valley left behind hundreds of caves, natural and man-made, that served as homes, animal shelter and grain stores. The many burial chambers found here form an important part of the Guanche exhibits of the Museo Canario in Las Palmas (➤ 84–85).

The area is little populated today, but the 50 or so inhabitants are probably the most direct descendants of this prehistoric world. They still farm the land, keep animals and live in the caves. They even park their cars in cave garages.

Learn more about the *barranco*, its history and ecology at the **Guayadeque Information Centre,** where a series of exhibits traces the story of the ravine and its people. The area's most famous restaurant is the Tagoror (➤ 59), right at the end of the *barranco* in a series of caves overlooking the valley. The stream beds under the trees make a pleasant and popular picnic spot at weekends.

✚ 22H ✉ Municipality of Agüimes: 30km (19 miles) south of Las Palmas, 28km (17 miles) northeast of Playa del Inglés 🍴 Several cafés in the *barranco*; Tagoror restaurant (➤ 59) ☎ 928 17 20 13 (€) 🚌 11 or 21 to Agüimes 🅿 Access on foot or by car from Agüimes (➤ 104) or Ingenio (➤ 107)
Guayadeque Information Centre
☎ 928 17 20 26 🕐 Tue–Sat 9–5, Sun 10–3

3 Casa de Colón

Once the governor's residence, this fine building now houses exhibits recalling the age of exploration.

When Juan Rejón founded the city of Las Palmas in 1478, among the first buildings he erected was a residence for the governor of the island. When Christopher Columbus arrived on the island on his first voyage of discovery in 1492, he presented his credentials to the governor and lodged in his house. This house, much restored and refurbished, is now the Casa de Colón.

The house is built around two elegant stone courtyards, decorated with Canarian balconies of

dense, dark tea pine wood. Twelve rooms on two floors contain the permanent exhibition; those dealing with the four voyages of Columbus to the New World are the most fascinating. A copy of the log of the first journey is left open at the page referring to the stop for repairs in Las Palmas. Given the direction of trade winds and ocean currents, the island was, and still is, a natural stopping-off point in any journey westwards. Subsequent generations have found it easier to travel between the Canaries and the Americas than to go in the other direction to mainland Spain. Cultural, social and familial ties have always been supplemented by ties of trade, and in times of economic trouble, many Canarios have found it more natural to emigrate to Latin America than to go to the mainland.

Highlights include a life-size reconstruction of the poop of the *Nina* and a copy of the 1494 Treaty of Tordesillas, which effectively divided the undiscovered world between Spain and Portugal. Among the intriguing displays are nautical maps, as fanciful as a child's drawing; navigational instruments, ingenious and inventive but looking hopelessly inadequate to the modern eye, and lists of the names of the seamen who manned the boats to the Americas. All the exhibits recall the magnitude of the explorers' task and the courage needed to fulfil it. There is also some excellent material on the history of Las Palmas.

➕ 11C or *Las Palmas 6h* ✉ Calle de Colón 1, Las Palmas
☎ 928 31 23 73 🕐 Mon–Fri 9–7, Sat–Sun 9–3 🎫 Free
🍴 Nearby 🚌 1, 2, 3

4 Cenobio de Valerón

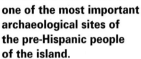

www.cenobiodevaleron.org

This network of around 300 caves is one of the most important archaeological sites of the pre-Hispanic people of the island.

It was once thought that the complex, in a rocky cliff a few miles east of the town of Santa María de Guía, usually known simply as Guía (► 173), was the abode of Guanche priestesses, or Harimaguadas, who served the god Alcorac; or that it housed young noblewomen in the period before marriage, when they were fed a calorie-rich diet in preparation for motherhood.

Now, scholars agree that the caves tunnelled out of the cliff-face by the island's early indigenous people were originally used as a fortified grain depository, indicating a culture with a high degree of social organization.

The caves, under a red-yellow basalt arch like the upper jaws of a great fish, appear from a distance like a colony of swallows' nests, made up of round and rectangular chambers. They are reached by winding, steep stairs cut into the rock, with the occasional platform.

Early writers described their astonishment on first seeing Cenobio de Valerón; the round arch, the intricate complex of caves connected by steps and

passages, and the towers which once stood at either side of the entrance overlooking the *barranco*. Its creation was no mean achievement by people who had no knowledge of metal and used only stones and animal bones as their tools.

The site has been enormously improved and stabilized, allowing visitors better access to the caves than for many years. You can climb up and explore the whole complex and there are plans for floodlit evening visits in the future – a superb way to experience this fascinating place.

✚ 6B ✉ Municipality of Santa María de Guía: 21km (13 miles) west of Las Palmas, 73km (45 miles) north of Playa del Inglés ☎ 618 60 78 96 🕐 Mon–Fri 9–2 ✋ Free, but guard is pleased with a small gratuity 🍴 None 🚌 103, 105 from Las Palmas

5 Dunas de Maspalomas

Spectacular sand dunes, part of a protected nature reserve, lie right in the middle of the busy tourist resort of Maspalomas.

Together with the Charco de Maspalomas – a freshwater lagoon behind the beach – and its associated palm grove, the dunes form an area of natural beauty and ecological importance to the south and west of Playa del Inglés and Maspalomas. Their sands, composed of finely ground shells, can reach a height of 10m (38ft) and are spread over an area of 328ha (810 acres), ending at the Fataga gorge.

Far from being composed of moving ridges shaped by wind, like the better known parts of the Sahara, these dunes are made up of what seems to be a host of sweetly contoured hillocks and surrounding valleys. It is a mildly surreal but loveable landscape.

When plans were launched in the early 1960s, by the Count of Vega Grande, local aristocrat and landowner, to start building tourist complexes on this coast, special pleas were made that the dunes should be protected from development. The luxury Hotel Grand Palace Maspalomas Oasis and the Maspalomas Golf Course were early lapses. But there are hopeful signs that this extraordinary natural asset, right in the centre of the greatest tourist concentration on the island, now has

enough champions to protect it from further depredation. Meanwhile, the dunes are advancing at the rate of one metre a year from left to right in the direction of the lighthouse.

In the *charco*, over 20 different species of birds have been observed in the past, and there are indications that the lagoon is being used increasingly as a stopping point during migration.

✚ 19M ✉ Maspalomas: 58km (36 miles) south of Las Palmas, 6km (4 miles) south of Playa del Inglés ❚❙ Plenty of refreshment places on and beside the beach (€–€€€) 🚌 Faro de Maspalomas is a busy bus terminal with many services to all areas. Bus 30 is a frequent direct service to Las Palmas ❓ Don't feed the fish in the *charco*. Left to themselves, they eat the mosquito larvae and keep this section of coast mosquito-free

6 Jardín Botánico Canario

www.jardincanario.org

This famous botancial garden in the Guiniguada *barranco* reveals all that is spiky and smooth, bizarre and beautiful of Gran Canarian flora.

The garden was opened in 1952, with the aim of preserving and displaying the many plant species endemic to the island. Its first director was the Swedish botanist Erik Sventenius, who did the preparatory groundwork of finding and classifying, planning and planting – a task assumed since 1974 by Dr David Bramwell.

The garden has two entrances, one at the top of the 150m-high (492ft) *barranco* and the other at its flat bottom, connected by paths and steps, and taking you through the many varieties of vegetation, planted at different levels. Here is your chance to walk among Canarian palms and the trees of the *laurasilva* (laurel) forest that once covered the island. The Jardín de las Islas displays all the most important species of plants of the archipelago, and the Cactus Garden has cacti from all over the world, with rare examples from South and Central America. Endangered species are tended in two nurseries with the aim of replanting them in their natural zones; there is also a library for study and research.

At the top of the garden are the circular lookout point and a white stone bust of historian and naturalist Don Jose de Viera y Clavijo (the garden's official name is Jardín Botánico Canario Viera y Clavijo). If you have managed to get this far up from the bottom of the *barranco*, reward yourself with some refreshment in the restaurant beside the garden entrance.

✚ 9D ✉ Tafira Alta: 7km (4 miles) south of Las Palmas, 53km (33 miles) northeast of Playa del Inglés ☎ 928 21 95 80 🕐 Daily 9–6 ♿ Free 🍴 Jardín Canario restaurant (€€) 🚌 301, 302, 303, 305. Ask the driver to drop you off at the gardens ❓ Occasional lectures

Playa de las Canteras

This wide hoop of sand, protected by a natural rock barrier, is one of Las Palmas's most prized amenities. The year-round pleasure of strolling or relaxing on these sands is shared by locals and visitors.

Backed by the hotels, shops and businesses of a major city, Las Canteras beach stretches in a golden curve, its comparatively shallow water warmed and sheltered from the wind by the presence of the inshore reef known as La Barra. A programme of improvements resulted in the planting of palm trees on the sands, and the re-building of a wide and attractive promenade, the Paseo de las Canteras, with attendant bars and restaurants, behind the beach.

Before mass air travel, visitors to Gran Canaria always arrived at Las Palmas by liner and tourism had its early beginnings in the north here, right behind Las Canteras beach.

Summer weekends find the beach almost as crowded as those in the south of the island; it attracts foreign visitors and local Canarios who prefer the slightly cooler, occasionally cloudy days of the north, where the prevailing northeast trade winds form clouds as they hit the mountains. There is a good choice of hotel accommodation, *pensions* and apartments, many of them with sea views. As for restaurants and nightlife, visitors will find all they expect from a beach resort, combined with the usual offerings of a sophisticated modern city; but in the end, the beach itself is the star.

🚌 10B or *Las Palmas 3a* 🍴 Cafés on and behind the beach (€–€€€) 🚌 1, 2, 3, 20, 21 🚢 Boats to Cádiz on Spanish mainland, jetfoil to Tenerife and ferries to all Canarian islands from passenger port
🛈 Parque de Santa Catalina ☎ 928 26 46 23

8 Puerto de Mogán

www.puerto-de-mogan.com

**Often referred to as 'Little Venice',
Puerto de Mogán is a low-rise resort in
the southwest of the island, complete with
an attractive marina.**

Until the 1980s this was simply a fishing village at
the mouth of the Barranco de Mogán, providing
shelter for a community of hippies and bohemians
as well as for local residents. The hippies moved
out – most unwillingly – as the first concrete mixers
arrived to create a new tourist *urbanización*.
Mutterings of rebellion against this development
were silenced here, however, as apartments with

prettily painted door and window surrounds, pedestrian-only streets, canals and bridges and, above all, hibiscus hedges and roof gardens tumbling with bougainvillaea, began to appear in the new Puerto de Mogán. Now, the resort is seen as an example of a tourist building style that does not violate the natural landscape.

Puerto de Mogán has a curved, grey, sandy beach protected by a breakwater, with sun beds. The focus, however, is the marina.

Throughout the day, passenger boats come and go between Mogán and other southern resorts. There are offers of fishing trips, submarine jaunts and sailing instruction. Chic shops and restaurants always seem full. Come evening, the day-trippers have gone and the town assumes a quiet, reflective air. Then, if a breeze stirs, you can hear the rigging rattling in the boats as you look up to the grandeur of the mountains behind.

✚ 14K ✉ Municipality of Mogán: 81km (50 miles) southwest of Las Palmas, 29km (18 miles) northwest of Playa del Inglés 🍴 Many cafés in resort (€–€€€) 🚌 1, 32 from Maspalomas/Playa del Inglés 🚢 Lineas Salmon boat to Puerto Rico, Arguineguín

Teror

Surrounded by hills, this is a beautiful showpiece town, as well as the spiritual heart of the island.

White houses with exposed grey stone, decoratively carved, dark wooden balconies and enchanting small patios hidden behind stern doors – this is the style of Canarian vernacular architecture, which is revealed at its best in Teror. Elegant and well preserved, the town also has the distinction of accommodating, in its splendid main square, the Basilica de Nuestra Señora del Pino – the Cathedral of Our Lady of the Pine, the patron saint of Gran Canaria. On this site and in a pine tree, so legend goes, the Virgin appeared to the first bishop of Gran Canaria, Juan Frías, in 1492.

The interior of the church is grand, with stone columns, a wooden coffered ceiling, a gilt *retablo* (altar-piece) shaped like the stern of a ship and, above the altar, the 15th-century statue of the Virgin on a silver litter. The Virgin is traditionally dressed in the richest robes, which are regularly changed. She

was also covered in a mass of precious jewels until 1975, when thieves made off with the treasure. They were never caught, and the incident is still a source of great anger and regret even to the most secular of Canarios.

Teror is an important place of pilgrimage to
islanders all through the year but particularly during
the festival of the Virgen del Pino on 8 September.
People converge on the town to offer prayers,
fulfil religious promises, bring gifts of fruit and
vegetables for the needy and – of course – to
dance and sing the nights away. Every other week
of the year, on Sunday mornings, a popular market
is held behind the church.

✚ 8D ✉ Municipality of Teror: 21km (13 miles) southwest
of Las Palmas, 77km (48 miles) north of Playa del Inglés
🍴 Several cafés (€–€€€) 🚌 216 from Las Palmas
❓ 8 Sep is the feast day of the Virgen del Pino, celebrated
throughout the island

10 Vegueta

Vegueta, the oldest part of Las Palmas, contains a concentration of the most historic sites of Gran Canaria. Nowhere else gives such an insight into the island's Spanish history.

The Catedral de Santa Ana (➤ 82) stands near the spot Juan Rejón chose to found the Ciudad Real de las Palmas (Royal City of the Palms), on 24 June, 1478. A few palms still flourish in the Plaza de Santa Ana, where children play among the pigeons. Two groups of bronze dogs, representing the animals after which, according to legend, the island is named, stand opposite the cathedral entrance.

Christopher Columbus stayed in the house behind the cathedral now called the Casa de Colón (➤ 40–41). The church where he prayed before setting off on his voyages, the Ermita de San Antonio Abad, is also in the Vegueta.

The Vegueta is a place of delightful smaller squares – among them the Plaza del Espiritu Santo and Plaza de Santo Domingo. Mansions line the streets, often decorated with traditional pine balconies – Calle de los Balcones, Calle León y Joven, Calle Herrería and Mendizábal are good examples. The Montesdeoca restaurant, in the street of the same name (➤ 60), is a revelation for its food and architecture.

Don't miss the excellent Museo Canario (➤ 84–85) for a glimpse of the life of the early aboriginal people of Gran Canaria. For modern life, visit the Mercado Municipal, the city's oldest market.

✚ 11C or *Las Palmas 5h*
🍴 Many cafés in area
(€–€€€) 🚌 1, 30 direct from Maspalomas
ℹ Parque Santa Catalina
☎ 928 26 46 23
🕔 Mon–Sat 8–2

Best things to do

Excellent restaurants

Amaiur (€€€)

This top restaurant serves superb food from the Spanish Basque region. Try the *lomo de merluza con almejas* – hake in clam sauce.
✉ Avenida Peréz Galdos 2, Las Palmas ☎ 928 37 07 17 🕐 Lunch, dinner; closed Sun

Bentayga (€€)

First-class restaurant using the best of local produce in local cuisine. The meat dishes – try lamb or goat – are highly recommended.
✉ Carretera del Centro 130, Monte Coello ☎ 928 355 186
🕐 8:30am–1:30am

El Herreño (€–€€)

There's a pleasant rustic feel to this excellent restaurant, whose owner comes from El Hierro, another of the islands in the archipelago. The menu reflects traditional Canarian cooking; the delicious roast pork is well worth trying.
✉ Calle Mendizábal 5 ☎ 928 31 05 13 🕐 9am–1am

Faneque (€€€)

This smart restaurant in the Hotel Puerto de las Nieves offers high-quality international and Canarian cooking, using both meat and fish.
✉ Avenida Alcalde José de Armas, Puerto de las Nieves ☎ 928 88 62 56 🕐 Lunch, dinner; closed Sun

Gorbea (€€€)

The restaurant of the Hotel Gloria Palace is open to non-residents for dinner. It offers stunning views from the ninth floor and excellent Basque cuisine with an emphasis on fish and seafood.

✉ Las Margaritas, San Agustín ☎ 928 12 85 00 🕐 Lunch Tue–Sat, dinner Mon–Sat; closed Sun, Jun

Guatiboa (€€€)

A top Canarian restaurant, part of a top hotel – the IFA Faro Maspalomas, just metres away from the beach – serves excellent food in sumptuous surroundings.

✉ Plaza de Faro 1, Maspalomas ☎ 928 14 22 14 🕐 Dinner

Jardín Canario (€€€)

A wonderful setting on the edge of the cliff above the botanical gardens. The food is excellent Canarian, the service is elegant.

✉ Carretera del Centro, km 7.200, Tafira Alta ☎ 928 351 091 🕐 Lunch, dinner

La Toja (€€€)

Excellent fish restaurant in two dining rooms in the centre of Playa del Inglés. *Caldo de pescado*, fish and vegetable soup, is delicious.

✉ Avenida Tirajana 17, Playa del Inglés ☎ 928 76 11 96 🕐 Lunch, dinner; closed Sun

Las Nasas (€€€)

A superb fish restaurant in an area renowned for fish eateries. Terrace to the beach.

✉ Calle Puerto de las Nieves 6, Agaete ☎ 928 89 86 50 🕐 Lunch, dinner

Tagoror (€€)

Praised as much for its location – high above the Guayadeque ravine – as for its food: strictly the best of Canarian cuisine.

✉ Montaña Las Tierras, 21, Guayadeque ☎ 928 17 20 13 🕐 Lunch, dinner

Good places to have lunch

Balcón de Zamora (€€)

Enjoy terrific views of Teror while eating good local dishes, including kid stew.

✉ Carretera a Vallesco km 8, Teror ☎ 928 61 80 42

Café Madrid (€)

Situated in the historic Hotel Madrid in Las Palmas. Excellent value menu of the day.

✉ Plaza de Cairasco 2, Las Palmas ☎ 928 36 06 64

Casa Montesdeoca (€€€)

Patio and ground floor of a restored mansion in the old town of Las Palmas. Wonderful atmosphere, great food.

✉ Montesdeoca 10, Las Palmas ☎ 928 33 34 66

Casa Romántica (€€)

Excellent international and Canarian food in Agaete; great ice-cream and fruit.

✉ Valle de Agaete, km 3.5, Agaete ☎ 928 89 80 84

Chipi-Chipi (€€)

Unpretentious restaurant in Playa del Inglés.

✉ Avenida Tirajana 19, Ed. Barbados 1, Playa del Inglés ☎ 928 76 50 88

Cofradía de Pescadores (€€)

A fishermen's co-operative with an island-wide reputation. Freshest of fish and seafood.

✉ Avenida del Muelle, Arguineguín ☎ 928 15 09 63

El Faro (€€)

Lovely location in a small lighthouse at the end of the fishing harbour of Puerto de Mogán. Excellent fish dishes.

✉ Puerto de Mogán ☎ 928 35 10 91

Gran Buffet Las Camelias (€)

A self-service restaurant at Playa des Inglés. Good variety.

 Avenida Tirajana 15, Playa des Inglés ☎ 928 76 02 36

Hipócrates (€€)

Vegetarian restaurant in the old town in Las Palmas. Good service.

✉ Calle Colón 4, Vegueta, Las Palmas ☎ 928 31 11 71

La Cantonera (€€–€€€)

Canarian dishes in a museum of Canarian rural life in Vega de San Mateo.

✉ Avenida Tinamar, Vega de San Mateo ☎ 928 33 13 74

Places to take the children

Aqualand

Day-long fun in pools and water slides, at this very popular water park (► 113).

✉ Carretera Palmitos Parque km 3, Maspalomas ☎ 928 14 05 25; www.aqualand.es ⏰ Summer daily 10–6; winter daily 10–5 🚌 45, 70 from Maspolamas

Cocodrilo Park

The largest collection of crocodiles in Europe can be seen in this park, 28km (17 miles) northwest of Playa del Inglés. Other animals are housed here, many rescued from cruelty and neglect. Crocodile and other shows throughout the day. Buses from main southern resorts and Las Palmas; enquire at local tourist office.

✉ Carretera Gral Los Corralillos km 5.5, Villa de Agüimes ☎ 928 78 47 25 ⏰ Sun–Fri 10–6

Escuela de Vela J Blanco

Sailing courses for groups or individuals; also boat trips.

✉ Playa de Puerto Rico, Puerto Rico ☎ 928 56 07 72

Holiday World

Everything for a great evening out for the family – roller coasters, arcades and plenty of restaurants (► 114).

✉ Avenida Touroperador Tui ☎ 928 73 04 98; www.holidayworld-maspalomas.com ⏰ Sun–Thu 9–2, Fri–Sat 9–6 🚌 25, 30, 32, 45

Mini-Tren

This miniature train covers a circular route at Playa del Inglés starting, and finishing, at the El Veril Comercial Centre on Avenida Italia. It gives small, tired legs a well-earned rest while revealing a different view of the world. The train usually leaves every 30 minutes for a 30-minute trip. The service is run privately and rather depends on the operator's mood.

✉ Playa del Inglés

Palmitos Parque

Although children love the performing parrots, this is much more than a parrot park. There is a great aquarium, and snack bars and cafés serving hamburgers and pizzas.

✉ Barranco de Chamoriscán ☎ 928 14 02 76 🕐 Daily 10–6 🚌 Free bus from Maspalomas; 45, 70 from Maspalomas

Sioux City

Wild West show with enough jail break-outs, gun-chases, bows and arrows and bullets (fake) for any young person to feel lucky (➤ 130).

✉ Barranco del Águila ☎ 928 76 25 73; www.siouxcity.es 🕐 Tue–Sun 10–5 🚌 Salcai bus 29

Spirit of the Sea

Enjoy a 2-hour dolphin search aboard this glass-bottomed catamaran with underwater microphones and cameras. You might even spot a whale! Part of the ticket price goes to research.

✉ Puerto Rico Harbour ☎ 928 56 22 29 🕐 10, 12:30, 3

Submarine Adventure

Journey to the bottom of the sea – well, almost. A 40-minute submarine trip to see, out of your very own porthole, a wreck and brilliant marine life.

✉ Pantalán Dique Sur, Puerto de Mogán ☎ 928 56 51 08 🕐 10, 11, 12, 1, 2, 3:30, 4:20, 5:10 🚌 Free bus from resorts

Activities

DEEP-SEA FISHING
Barakuda Dos
High seas fishing trip. Reserve at least two days ahead.
✉ Puerto Rico ☎ 676 47 96 87; www.barakudados.com ⏰ Daily 9–3, 3:30–7:30

DIVING
Dive Academy
Dive centre with its own pool for tuition; PADI accredited.
✉ Club Amigos del Atlantico C/Lajilla s/n, Arguineguín ☎ 928 73 61 96; www.diveacademy-grancanaria.com ⏰ Tue–Sun 9–6

GO-KARTING
Gran Karting Club
Not just for adults or big kids, this go-kart track – the largest in Spain – even caters for children under five (➤ 128).
✉ Carretera General del Sur km 46, San Agustín ☎ 928 15 71 90
⏰ Summer daily 11–10; winter daily 10–9

GOLF
Campo de Golf
Close to dunes and palm groves, this is a splendidly sited golf course: 18 holes, par 73, 6,220m (6,750yds) course.
✉ Avenida Neckerman s/n, Maspalomas ☎ 928 76 25 81 🚌 30

HORSE RIDING
Happy Horse
One- to three-hour excursions into the southern hills for novice and experienced riders; tuition at riding school also available. Pickups from hotels.

✉ Lomo de la Presa Calderin Alto ☎ 679 86 70 57; www.happy-horse.org

MOUNTAIN BIKING
Free Motion
Bike rental from one to six days, plus a good selection of accompanied bike tours to suit all levels of fitness. They also organize hiking excursions.

✉ Avenida Alfereces Provisionales s/n, Playa del Inglés ☎ 928 77 77 49; www.free-motion.net

SAILING
Atlantic Islands Sail Training Centre
RYA-accredited sailing school offering everything from two-day learn-to-sail courses to advanced yachtmaster certificates.

✉ Calipso, Pasaje de los Pescadores 9, Puerto de Mogán ☎ 928 56 59 31; www.ryasailingschools.com

WALKING
Canariaventura
Guided walk departs Wednesdays at 9am. Also offers climbing, canyoning and bungee-jumping.

✉ Centro Comercial Eurocenter, Planta 2, Local 29, Playa del Inglés ☎ 928 76 61 68; www.canariaventura.com

WINDSURFING
F2 Surfcenter Dunkerbeck
Windsurf school for beginners and those with advanced skills.

✉ Plaza de Hibiscus, Playa del Águila, San Agustín ☎ 928 76 29 78; www.dunkerbeck-windsurfing.com

a walk around the historic district of Las Palmas

This walk starts at Calle Mayor de Triana, the shopping street that leads down to Vegueta, the old city. After visiting Vegueta, it returns to historic Plaza de Cairasco.

Walk south from Emita de San Telmo (▶ 89) on pedestrian-only Calle Mayor de Triana. Note the art nouveau buildings starting at No 98. Finally, angle left at the statue of Juan Negrín. At the major highway, go one block left to Teatro Pérez Galdós. Return and cross over to the market (Mercado de Las Palmas), on the left. Continue on along Calle Mendizábal, then right up Calle de los Balcones.

Here, the island's artistic heritage is on display at CAAM (Centro Atlántico de Arte Moderno, ▶ 84).

In Plaza del Pilar turn right, following the east side of Casa de Colón. At the next small square, the Church of San Antonio Abad is to the right, and further down is the Montesdeoca restaurant (▶ 60). Return and follow the north side of Casa de Colón

(entrance on left). Continue straight ahead, with the cathedral to your left, into Plaza de Santa Ana and turn left, passing the cathedral façade.

The cathedral museum (➤ 82) is 25m (27yds) left at the next turning, in Espiritu Santo.

Retrace your steps to the end of Espiritu Santo. Turn left into Calle Reloj and walk to Calle Dr Chil. Turn right. Passing the Museo Canario on the left, continue 60m (65yds) up Calle Dr Chil, then angle sharply back into Plaza de Santa Ana. From the cathedral front, exit left down Calle Obispo Codina. Cross the highway and go straight on into Plaza de Cairasco.

Recover with a drink or lunch outside the Hotel Madrid, where Franco spent the night on the eve of the insurrection of the generals in 1936.

Distance 2.5km (1.5 miles)
Time 1.5 hours strolling, four hours with visits to attractions
Start point Calle Mayor de Triana
End point Plaza de Cairasco
Lunch Café Madrid (€; ➤ 60). Also many cafés and bars in market area

Museums and art galleries

Casa Museo León y Castillo

This museum in Telde is the former home of Juan de León y Castillo, the engineer who built the harbour at Las Palmas (➤ 176).

✉ Calle León y Castillo 43–5 ☎ 928 69 13 77 🕓 Mon–Fri 8–8, Sat–Sun 10–1 ⬚ Free 🍴 Near museum (€–€€)

Casa Museo de Pérez Galdós

This museum and study centre in Las Palmas is the birthplace of the Canarian novelist, playwright and social critic, Benito Pérez Galdós (➤ 82).

✉ Calle Cano 6 ☎ 928 36 69 76; www.casamuseoperezgaldos.com 🕓 Mon–Fri 9–7 ⬚ Free, conducted tour on the hour 🚌 1, 11

Casa Museo Tomás Morales

This museum is the birthplace of the poet and doctor, Tomás Morales, in the plaza now named after him in the northern town of Moya (➤ 169).

✉ Plaza de Tomás Morales 1 ☎ 928 62 02 17 🕓 Mon–Fri 9–8, Sat 10–8, Sun 10–2 ⬚ Free

Centro Atlántico de Arte Moderno (CAAM)

Modern art gallery in Las Pamas showing the work of contemporary, mostly Spanish, and some Canarian, artists (➤ 84).

✉ Calle de los Balcones 9–11 ☎ 928 31 18 24; www.caam.net 🕓 Tue–Sat 10–9, Sun 10–2 ⬚ Free 🍴 Cafés/restaurants (€–€€€) 🚌 1, 2, 3

Mundo Aborigen

This open-air museum (➤ 116) re-creates a Stone-Age settlement, with life-sized figures of early Guanches, spread across the upper hillsides of Barranco de Fataga.

✉ Carretera de Fataga ☎ 928 17 22 95 🕓 Daily 9–6 ⬚ Moderate 🍴 Café and souvenir shop on premises (€€) 🚌 18 from Maspalomas

Museo Canario

In this excellent museum, dedicated to the prehistory of Gran
Canaria, you get a glimpse of the lives of the aboriginal people
who inhabited the island during the Spanish conquest (➤ 84–85).
✉ Calle Dr Verneau 2 ☎ 928 33 68 00; www.elmuseocanario.com
🕐 Mon–Fri 10–8, Sat–Sun 10–2 🖐 Inexpensive 🍴 Good cafés nearby
(€–€€€) 🚌 1, 2, 3

Museo Castillo de la Fortaleza

Museo Castillo de la Fortaleza in Santa Lucía is a former
farmhouse containing pre-Spanish artefacts (➤ 152–153).
✉ Calle Tomás Arroyo Cardoso ☎ 928 79 80 07 🕐 Daily 9–5
🖐 Inexpensive 🍴 Restaurant in museum (€€)

Museo Elder

This excellent museum of science and technology has over 200
exhibits all labelled in English as well as Spanish (➤ 85).
✉ Parque Santa Catalina ☎ 828 01 18 28; www.museoelder.org
🕐 Tue–Sun 10–8 (summer 11–9). Closed Mon and some public hols
🖐 Moderate (IMAX cinema extra) 🍴 Café in museum (€) 🚌 1, 2, 3

Museo Néstor

The life work of the island's most famous painter, Néstor Martín
Fernández de la Torre (1887–1938) is displayed in this museum in
the Pueblo Canario (➤ 86).
✉ Pueblo Canario ☎ 928 24 51 35; www.museonestor.com 🕐 Tue–Sat
10–8, Sun and hols 10:30–2:30 🖐 Moderate 🍴 Café in Pueblo Canario (€)
🚌 1

Museo de Piedras y Artesanía Canaria

This Museum of Rocks and Canarian Handicraft in Ingenio displays
an indifferent collection of rocks but excellent handicrafts (➤ 107).
✉ Camino Real de Gando 1 ☎ 928 78 11 24 🕐 Mon–Sat 8–6:30 🖐 Free
🍴 Small refreshment bar (€)

Best places to stay

Anfi del Mar (€€)
Luxury aparthotel with every comfort and amenity, swimming pools, restaurants, tropical gardens, marina and a beach of white Caribbean sand. Exceptional value.

✉ Barranco de la Verga, Arguineguín ☎ 928 150 059; www.anfi.com

Casa de los Camellos (€€)
Lovely rural hotel renovated from a 300-year-old stone barn set around courtyards and gardens. It has 12 rooms.

✉ Calle Progreso 12, Agüimes ☎ 928 78 50 03

Hotel Dunas La Canaria (€€€)
Right on the beach in the south of the island, you can enjoy year-round sunshine at what is regarded as one of the best hotels on the island. Every room has a sea view, service is discreet and the spa and pool are state of the art.

✉ Barranco de la Verga, Arguineguín ☎ 928 15 04 00; www.hotelesdunas.com

Hotel Las Tirajanas (€€€)
This lovely mountain hotel has wonderful views, large airy rooms, a restaurant serving local specialities and a beautiful pool.

✉ Calle Oficial Mayor José Rubio, San Bartolomé de Tirajana ☎ 928 12 30 00; www.hotel-lastirajanas.com

Hotel Puerto de las Nieves (€€€)
Luxury hotel with many facilities including sauna, Jacuzzi and therapy treatments. Close to beach.

✉ Calle José de Armas, Agaete ☎ 928 88 62 56

Hotel Taurito Princess (€€€)
A splendid hotel above the beach just outside Puerto de Mogán. Great views of garden, pool and coast.

✉ Playa de Taurito, Mogán ☎ 928 56 53 10

IFA Faro Maspalomas (€€€)

Luxury hotel metres away from the lighthouse after which it is named. The sea views are glorious, the hotel restaurant Guatiboa (➤ 59) is one of the best on the island and guests are entitled to a discount on the Maspalomas golf course green fees.

✉ Plaza del Faro, Maspalomas ☎ 928 14 29 91

La Casa Roja (€€–€€€)

In a beautiful situation, this 19th-century mansion was renovated into a country hotel.

✉ Calle Doctor Chil 20, Valle de Agaete km 4, Agaete ☎ 928 89 81 45

Palacio Dunamar (€€€)

An incomparable position on the beach and the views from sea-facing rooms make this hotel special. Swimming pool and squash courts.

✉ Avenida de Helsinki 8, Playa del Inglés ☎ 928 76 50 11

Riu Grand Palace Maspalomas Oasis (€€€)

Undoubtedly the most luxurious hotel in the south, the Oasis is situated on the beach, beside the dunes and surrounded by palms.

✉ Plaza de las Palmeras, Playa de Maspalomas ☎ 928 14 14 48; www.riu.com

Best souvenirs to buy

BASKETWORK
FEDAC
The Fundación para la Etnografía y el Desarollo de la Artesania Canaria is a non-profit public trust for the development of Canarian handicrafts and has two outlets on the island. This branch in Las Palmas sells carved bone-handled knives *(naifes)*, pottery, traditional musical instruments and basketwork.

✉ Calle Domingo J Navarro 7 ☎ 928 36 96 61; www.fedac.org

CANARIAN CIGARS
Juan Marquez
Cigars and cigarettes of all lengths and thicknesses, including those from the island of La Palma.

✉ Calle Ripoche 1, Las Palmas ☎ 928 26 56 35

DECORATED CANARIAN KNIVES
Guía, Gáldar and Telde villages
Traditional craftsmen, especially in these three villages, make *cuchillos Canarios* (Canarian knives), an essential tool for every Canarian farmer and collectors' pieces, due to their decorated handles.

EMBROIDERY WORK
Higmara
The specialty of the shop is embroidered shawls.

✉ 22 León y Castillo, Las Palmas ☎ 928 26 94 87

FELT HATS
Tienda FEDAC de Playa del Inglés
All manner of Canarian handcrafted items, including traditional black sombreros *(cachorro canario)*.

✉ Avenida de España/Avenida de los Estados Unidos
☎ 928 77 24 45

MUSICAL INSTRUMENTS
Orbis
Sr Miguel Santana Cruz specializes in off-the-peg and custom-made *timples*, a small Canarian guitar.

✉ Calle Mayor de Triana 51, Las Palmas ☎ 928 36 81 48

PLANT PRODUCTS
Aloe Vera de Canarias
The Canary Islands' most famous plant product is aloe vera, which is used in cosmetics, diet and pharmaceutical products. For high quality, buy it from a reputable outlet, such as Aloe Vera de Canarias.

✉ Calle Doctor Miguel Rosa 37, Las Palmas ☎ 928 88 46 35

POTTERY
Tienda FEDAC
Look here for Canarian pottery – hand-turned and unglazed.

✉ Avenida de España/Avenida de los Estados Unidos, Playa del Inglés ☎ 928 77 24 45

RUM
Destilerías Arehucas
Come here for rum, produce of Arucas. See barrels signed by King Juan Carlos and singer Tom Jones and then have a free tasting of rum and liqueurs.

✉ Lugar Era de San Pedro 2, Arucas ☎ 928 62 49 00

WALKING STICKS
Roberto Ramirez
This is the place for walking sticks that are carved, sculpted, inlaid, bound and decorated until they become collectors' pieces.

✉ Calle Mateos 9, Arucas ☎ 928 60 14 65

Places to be entertained

Bachira
Loud and popular fashionable venue with house and dance music.

✉ Centro Comercial Plaza, Playa del Inglés ⏱ All night

Camel Bar
On Calle León y Castillo, a popular club venue not far from the old part of the city. You can eat a meal before dancing the night away.

✉ Calle León y Castillo 389, Las Palmas ☎ 928 27 23 06 ⏱ Mon–Sat 9pm–4am

Casino de las Palmas
The smartest place on the island to risk your fortune, or watch someone else risk theirs on black jack, *chemin de fer*, baccarat, roulette, etc. Formal dress obligatory. Take your passport with you.

✉ Santa Catalina Hotel, Parque Doramas ☎ 928 23 39 08 www.casinolaspalmas.com ⏱ Sun–Thu 8pm–4am, Fri–Sat 8pm–5am

El Coto
As you would expect of a disco in the Hotel Melia, in the middle of Playa de las Canteras, El Coto is elegant and refined – even on a Saturday night. The music is international/Latin American.

✉ Calle Gomera 6, Las Palmas ☎ 928 26 76 00

Floridita
A large popular restaurant/bar in the Triana district. Locals love the Cuban rhythms.

✉ Remedios 10–12, Las Palmas ☎ 928 43 17 40

Gran Casino Costa Meloneras

Southern Gran Canaria's casino is your best bet for a big night out. There's an elegant restaurant, a spectacular nightly floor show and black jack, roulette and poker, as well as slot machines.

✉ Avenida Mar Mediterráneo, Maspalomas ☎ 928 14 39 09 (casino); 928 14 39 69 (booking for floor show); www.grancasinocostameloneras.com

Guasqueas

Smart and lively venue for all age groups to see top performers. Good jazz and Latin American music.

✉ Calle San Pedro 2, near Triana, Las Palmas ☎ 928 37 00 46 🕓 From 10:30pm–late

Heaven

Gay and straight dance club with a hot reputation.

✉ Third floor, Yumbo Centrum, Maspalomas 🕓 All night

Pacha

Smart, popular disco that's been around for a while. Giant video screen and live music on the terrace.

✉ Avenida Provisionales 10, Playa del Inglés ☎ 928 76 81 77

Pueblo Canario

Many cultures have contributed to the folk dancing styles of Gran Canaria, not least the Spanish, Portuguese and Latin American. The *isa* is a lively, energetic dance; the *folia* is slower and more languorous, and *el canario* is a group dance. All are performed once a week at the Pueblo Canario, accompanied by music played on traditional instruments. The folk costumes, now worn on rare formal occasions, differ from village to village, but they are all splendidly colourful.

✉ Parque Doramas ☎ 928 242 985 🕓 Performances: Sun 11:30am 🚌 1

Best places to shop

Artesanía Canaria
Buy Canarian products made from simple and pure materials including clay, wool, linen and iron. Two branches in the town.
✉ Parque Doramas, Fataga ☎ 928 24 39 11

Centro Comercial Atlántico
It's worth heading up the coast to this major shopping mall in Vecindario, featuring such names as Zara, Mango, Cortefiel and Bata. There's a huge Carrefour, food court and multiplex cinema.
✉ Calle Adargoma, Vecindario ☎ 928 79 40 74

Doramas
Mouthwatering biscuits and cakes, including the traditional *mimos* and *suspiros*.
✉ Calle General Franco 19, Moya ☎ 928 62 00 80

El Corte Inglés
Large department store on both sides of the street. You can buy anything from cheese to perfume, clothes, furniture and books.
✉ Avenida Mesa y Lopez 18, Las Palmas ☎ 928 26 30 00

Faro 2
Regarded as the most upmarket place in the whole San Agustín/Playa del Inglés/Maspalomas complex. Faro 2 is one of three centres in Maspalomas, the others being Oasis and Veradero.
✉ Avenida Touroperador Holland, Maspalomas ☎ 928 76 91 97

La Atalaya
This village has long been a centre of pottery production. There is a strong sense of preserving traditional techiniques and the ALUD (Association of Professionals of La Loza of La Atalaya) has a programme of continued research and teaching as well as organizing the exhibition and sale of items of pottery.
✉ Camino de la Picota 11 ☎ 928 28 82 70

La Bodeguilla Juananá

A craft shop-cum-restaurant selling the best – that is, the most authentic – Canarian produce, be it ceramic bowls or local cheeses.

✉ Puerto de Mogán, local 390 ☎ 928 56 50 44

La Librería

The best bookshop in Las Palmas is run by the island government and stocks a wide range.

✉ Calle Cano 24, Las Palmas ☎ 928 38 15 39

Mercado de Vegueta

The oldest general market in Las Palmas, where you can find fish, meat, fruit and vegetables – the variety of potatoes is astonishing. The market is surrounded by lively bars and *churrerias* – stalls selling *churros* (a traditional Spanish breakfast).

✉ Calle Mendizábal, Las Palmas

Yumbo Centrum

This is the biggest commercial centre in the resort. Other centres are Aguila Roja, Alohe, Anexo 11, Cita, El Veril, Gran Chaparral, Kasbah; La Sandia, Metro, Plaza de Maspalomas and Tropical.

✉ Avenida de Los Estados Unidos 54, Playa del Inglés ☎ 928 76 41 96

Exploring

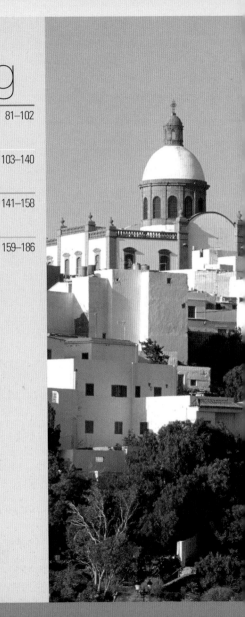

The name 'Canaria' first appeared on a Spanish map in 1339. Christopher Columbus (1451–1506), on several of his voyages across the Atlantic, put in at Gran Canaria. The aboriginal people living on the island at that time came to be known as the Guanches. Their legacy is everywhere and they have left their mark on the physical appearance and names of many present-day islanders, as well as the sports that they enjoy.

While sun and sea are the main attractions of Gran Canaria, peace and quiet can be found at beaches on the northwestern tip, the reservoirs of Chira, and Soria and Cueva de las Niñas in the the centre, or walking in the more remote areas. Gran Canaria is a also botanist's delight, with a wide variety of vegetation, including the exotic dragon tree *(Dracaena draco)*, the botanical symbol of Gran Canaria.

Las Palmas

Las Palmas is the capital city of Gran Canaria and also capital of the province bearing the same name. It is the largest city in the Canary Islands, lying like a long (14km/9 miles) and narrow ribbon on the island's northeast tip, barred from the sea by a highway.

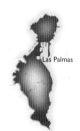

There are four distinct zones of interest in Las Palmas: Vegueta, Triana, Ciudad Jardín and Playa de las Canteras. Vegueta, the monumental historic centre, adjoins Triana, a commercial district with fine examples of modernista architecture, a style of flowing curves and curious shapes. Ciudad Jardín (Garden City) is

a leafy suburb created by British merchants in the 19th century, where you will find Parque Doramas; and a quick hop across town takes you to Parque Santa Catalina and the splendid beach, Playa de las Canteras.

Nowhere in Spain is the traditional pre-Lenten Carnival celebrated with as much gusto as in the Canary Islands, and for nearly three weeks in February Las Palmas is one giant party, with acrobats, clowns, magicians, brass bands, salsa music, fireworks and riotous fancy-dress parades.

✠ 10B

ℹ See page 30

CASA DE COLÓN

Best places to see, ➤ 40–41.

CASA MUSEO DE PÉREZ GALDÓS

The birthplace of the Canarian novelist, playwright and social critic Benito Pérez Galdós is now a museum and study centre. Born in 1843 in this fine town house built around a tiny patio, Pérez Galdós pursued a distinguished literary career on the Spanish mainland. Although he studied the influence of the old Guanche language on contemporary usage while he was a student, the island never featured in his writing. Exhibits include the author's books, furniture made to his own design, a portrait of him by Sorolla and a re-creation of his study in Santander.

www.casamuseoperezgaldos.com

🏠 *Las Palmas 6g* ✉ Calle Cano 6 ☎ 928 36 69 76 🕐 Mon–Fri 9–7
🎟 Free; conducted tour on the hour 🚌 1, 11

CATEDRAL DE SANTA ANA

A mixture of Gothic, Renaissance, baroque and neoclassical styles reflects the fact that, although this cathedral was begun in 1497, it has only recently been completed and cleared of scaffolding. The west front, designed by local architect Luján Pérez and completed in the early 19th century, faces the palm-lined square of Santa Ana and the two groups of bronze dogs, which some speculate, gave the island its name (from the Latin *canis*, 'dog'). Because of building works, the cathedral is reached through the **Museo Diocesano de Arte Sacro** (Diocesan Museum of Sacred Art). Here there is a fine, if limited, collection of polychrome sculpture; the building and courtyard a real reward in themselves.

🏠 *Las Palmas 6h* ✉ Plaza Santa Ana 🕐 Cathedral: daily 10–8; tower 9.15–6 🎟 Moderate 🚌 1, 2, 3

Museo Diocesano de Arte Sacro

✉ Calle Espíritu Santo 20 ☎ 928 31 49 89 🕐 Mon–Fri 10–4:30, Sat 10–1:30

CENTRO ATLÁNTICO DE ARTE MODERNO (CAAM)

This sparkling white gallery, housed in a grand mansion in one of the city's most picturesque streets, opened in 1989 and shows the work of contemporary artists. This is a surprisingly effective modern environment in an antique setting. Exhibitions are varied; the director is the noted sculptor Martin Chirino.

www.caam.net

⊞ *Las Palmas 6h* ✉ Calle de los Balcones 9–11 ☎ 928 31 18 24
🕓 Tue–Sat 10–9, Sun 10–2 🎟 Free
🍴 Cafés/restaurants in Vergueta (€–€€€)
🚌 1, 2, 3

MUSEO CANARIO

In this museum you can glimpse the lives of the neolithic people who inhabited the island. Exhibits show that they lived in caves, as well as stone houses. They kept livestock and grew cereal; they ground grain with millstones and used pestles and mortars. They mummified their dead – see the long gallery of skulls, skeletons and mummies wrapped in *junco* (cloth made of reeds) and goatskin. They were expert at leather and cane work and made fine pottery without the benefit of the wheel. Although they had no written language, they left many examples of rock engravings depicting humans, animals and geometric symbols. The famous Painted Cave of Gáldar (➤ 168), one of the island's best archaeological sites, is reproduced in this museum.

The islanders were ruled by kings, or *guanartemes*, practised sports such as wrestling and cross-stick fighting (still popular among modern Canarios), and, according to contemporary accounts, they loved music and dancing. The first Europeans described the inhabitants as generous, simple and trusting. However, when it became clear that their visitors, armed with superior weapons (the Guanches had no knowledge of metal and had never seen a horse), were intent on invading and enslaving them, they resisted them with courage and skill.

www.elmuseocanario.com

✚ *Las Palmas 6h* ✉ Calle Dr Verneau 2 ☎ 928 33 68 00 🕐 Mon–Fri 10–8, Sat–Sun 10–2. Closed public hols ✋ Inexpensive 🍴 Good cafés nearby in Vergueta (€–€€€) 🚌 1, 2, 3

MUSEO ELDER

In this excellent museum of science and technology you'll find a fascinating approach to subjects such as mathematics, biology and technology. You can watch chicks hatch, go inside an F5 plane, explore sound and waves and learn about energy. The IMAX cinema has screenings in English.

www.museoelder.org

✚ *Las Palmas 4a* ✉ Parque Santa Catalina ☎ 828 01 18 28 🕐 Tue–Sun 10–8 (summer 11–9). Closed Mon and some public hols ✋ Moderate (IMAX cinema extra) 🍴 Café in museum (€) 🚌 1, 2, 3

MUSEO NÉSTOR

This museum, in the Pueblo Canario, displays the work of the island's most famous painter, Néstor Martín Fernández de la Torre (1887–1938). His best-known work, *Atlantic Sea Poem* (two series of four canvases), is a celebration of the island's ocean environment. Néstor was pre-occupied by the effect of modern development on the island, reacting with angry denunciations and positive projects for retaining all that is best in Canarian architecture. The Pueblo Canario itself is part of his resistance.

www.museonestor.com

🔹 *Las Palmas 4d* ✉ Pueblo Canario ☎ 928 24 51 35 ⏰ Tue–Sat 10–8, Sun and hols 10:30–2:30 ✋ Moderate 🍴 Café in Pueblo Canario (€) 🚌 1

PARQUE DORAMAS

This shady park, in the middle of Ciudad Jardín, contains the Hotel Santa Catalina, the Pueblo Canario and the Museo Néstor. Doramas, after whom the park was named, was the last Guanche king of Eastern Gran Canaria. In 1481, on Montaña de Arucas, he challenged the Spaniards to single combat and killed his rival with a javelin throw, but was fatally wounded himself. The Spanish and Guanche forces then joined in battle, but it was soon over. This was the final act of armed resistance against the Spaniards. Many of Doramas's followers later hurled themselves off the cliffs, an event commemorated in the wild bronze sculpture in the hotel garden.

🔹 *Las Palmas 4d* ✉ Ciudad Jardín ⏰ Daily ✋ Free 🍴 Café in Pueblo Canario and Hotel Santa Catalina (€–€€€) 🚌 1

PARQUE SANTA CATALINA

The liveliest public space in Las Palmas, this park – which is really more of a city square – is surrounded by pavement cafés. This is where you can see Las Palmas at its most cosmopolitan, as Korean and Russian seamen mingle with African street-traders and tourists from northern Europe, while Canarios gather to play games of chess and dominoes at the café tables. Perfumeries and bazaar-like shops fill up the side-streets, which also act as a red-light district by night. This is home to the Museo Elder (➤ 85). You will find the city's main tourist information office in a traditional Canarian building at the corner of the square.

➕ *Las Palmas 4a* ✉ Santa Catalina 🍴 Many cafés around (€–€€€)
🚌 1, 2, 3
ℹ Tourist Information Office ☎ 928 26 46 23

PARQUE SAN TELMO

The most appealing of all Las Palmas's parks, this is the one most people see first as they step out of the bus station. The park was initially built on the site of a small cove but the bus station and motorway have forced the sea to recede. A shady square full of tall palms and benches, this park is famous for its kiosk café, decorated in *modernista* style with ceramic tiles from Manises, and for its small church, the Ermita de San Telmo (patron saint of fishermen). The church, decorated with a little Canarian balcony, was rebuilt in the 17th century after destruction by Dutch pirates. Inside, there is a fine *artesonado* (wooden panelled) ceiling and a baroque retablo (altar-piece). On the west side of the park, a stern neoclassical building guarded by soldiers is the Spanish army headquarters in the Canary Islands. It was from here that General Franco, on a visit to Gran Canaria, announced his opposition to the Republican government on 18 July 1936 and broadcast a rallying call to his troops, thus beginning the Spanish Civil War from which he emerged the victor in 1939. A bus terminus and taxi-stand make this park an important communications point.

✛ *Las Palmas 6g* ✉ Corner of Calle Bravo Murillo and Avenida Rafael Cabrera 🍴 Many cafés around (€–€€€) 🚌 1, 11, 41 ❓ Church open only during services

PLAYA DE LAS ALCARAVANERAS

Las Palmas's second town beach after Las Canteras is a fine sweep of golden sand which has suffered from its proximity to the port and the marina. Those suspecting the cleanliness of the water use the beach for sunbathing and beach football. Locals, self-styled 'fans of Las Alcaravaneras', would not go elsewhere.

✛ *Las Palmas 4b* ✉ Alcaravaneras 🍴 Snack bars on beach (€) 🚌 1, 2, 3

PLAYA DE LAS CANTERAS

Best places to see, ➤ 48–49.

a walk around the parks and gardens

This pleasant walk around the delightful old city of Las Palmas takes you to the Pueblo Canario (Canarian Village) (► 92), Parque Doramas (► 86), the Ciudad Jardín (City Garden) and the modern shopping centre, before heading northwards to the lively Parque Santa Catalina (► 87).

Start under the huge ficus tree to the southern side of the Pueblo Canario.

Within the pueblo, the fine Museo Néstor (► 86) is to the right, the shops in front, and the outdoor café/restaurant to the left. Beyond the pueblo is the Hotel Santa Catalina, which is worth a visit to admire its beautiful gardens.

Leave the hotel directly behind you, crossing the park (past the Doramas monument) to Calle León y Castillo.

Turn left here, then second left up Avenida Alejandro Hidalgo. Take the first right into Calle Lord Byron, and go through Ciudad Jardín to the far side. Take the first left up Jose Miranda Guerra, then the second right into Leopardi and continue, angling right along Calle de Brasil. Take the third left (Calle Rafael Almírez), one block, to turn right on to Pio XII.

The route is now linear until its last stages, with many variations of neighbourhood (and changes of road name). The first stretch is dull, but after about 10 minutes the route reaches a produce market, to the right, and then intersects with the major shopping street, Avenida Mesa y Lopez (the department store El Corte Inglés and Marks & Spencer are both your right).

Cross over the street and continue straight along it as it quickly becomes Calle Tomás Miller.

Playa de las Canteras (➤ 48–49), the town's fine beach, lies straight ahead.

The walk then turns right two blocks before the beach, up pedestrian Ripoche to Parque Santa Catalina with the excellent Museo Elder (➤ 85).

Distance 1.5km (0.8 miles)
Time 30 mins strolling; 3 hours with attractions and shopping
Start point Southern entrance to Pueblo Canario ✚ *Las Palmas 4e*
End point Parque Santa Catalina ✚ *Las Palmas 4a*
Lunch Start with lunch at Bodegón in Pueblo Canario (€)

PUEBLO CANARIO

The Pueblo Canario (Canarian Village) is an attempt to preserve, re-create and display the best of Canarian architecture. A small group of buildings on the edge of Parque Doramas (► 86), based on the plans of the artist, Néstor Martín Fernández de la Torre, was erected after his death. There is a pretty courtyard, with outdoor café tables, the restored Church of Santa Catalina, and a covered arcade of small shops selling Canarian handicraft – open threadwork tablecloths, musical instruments and decorated Canarian knives.

✚ *Las Palmas 4e* ✉ Parque Doramas 🕑 Tue–Fri 10–8, Sun 10:30–2:30
🍴 Pueblo Canario Bodegón (€€) 🚌 1 ❓ Performances of traditional music and dance Sun 11:30am

TEATRO PÉREZ GALDÓS

Set on the edge of the busy carriageway that divides Triana from Vegueta, this theatre was designed by the architect Miguel Martín Fernández de la Torre and the murals (of Apollo and the Muses) painted by his brother Néstor in a style that shocked respectable theatregoers when they were revealed.

✚ *Las Palmas 6h*
✉ Plaza de Stagno/Lentini 1 ☎ 928 36 15 09
🍴 Cafés in area (€–€€€) 🚌 1, 11

VEGUETA

Best places to see, ► 54–55.

HOTELS

Astoria (€€)

A modern hotel near Playa de las Canteras with terrace, swimming pool, gym and squash courts.

✉ Calle Fernándo Guanarteme 54 ☎ 928 22 27 50; www.bullhotels.com

Atlanta (€€)

Good facilities in this friendly hotel, only a few minutes from the beach. All rooms are air-conditioned.

✉ Calle Alfredo L Jones 37 ☎ 928 27 80 00; www.atlantacanarias.com

Cantur (€€)

Comfortable, 1960s-built hotel with terrace; many rooms with view of Playa de las Canteras. Breakfast included.

✉ Calle Sagasta 26 ☎ 928 27 30 00; www.hotelcantur.com

Colón (€€)

An apartment block situated at the beach end of this busy street. Go for the sea-view rooms.

✉ Calle Alfredo Jones 45 ☎ 928 22 08 76

Concorde (€€€)

A modern hotel that is comfortable and well-run, situated close to Canteras beach and Parque Santa Catalina. Swimming pool.

✉ Calle Tomás Miller 85 ☎ 928 26 27 50; www.hotelconcorde.org

Fataga (€€)

A middle-range hotel in the business area of the city within easy walking distance of both Canteras and Alcaravaneras beaches. It has 92 rooms.

✉ Calle Nestor de la Torre 21 ☎ 900 50 69 04; www.partner-hotels.com

Faycan (€)

Moderately priced, clean and comfortable hotel with 61 rooms in a central situation.

✉ Calle Nicolas Estevanez 61 ☎ 928 27 06 54

Hotel AC Gran Canaria (€€)

Formerly luxurious but now in need of renovation work, this hotel offers glorious views. Solarium and swimming pool on site.

✉ Calle Eduardo Benot 3 ☎ 928 26 61 00; www.ac-hotels.com

Hotel Idafe (€)

Basic but clean, this centrally located hotel is close to the beach.

✉ Calle Nicolas Estevanez 49 ☎ 928 26 56 70

Hotel Igramar Canteras (€€)

Only 50m (54yds) from the beach, this comfortable hotel offers access for visitors with disabilities.

✉ Calle Columbia 12 ☎ 928 47 29 60; www.igramar.com

Hotel Imperial Playa (€€€)

Many of the rooms in this eight-storey hotel overlook Las Canteras beach, and it's just a few steps down to the sands. The interior is comfortable and services and facilities are what you would expect from a hotel that caters for both business travellers and tourists.

✉ Calle Ferreras 1 ☎ 928 46 88 54; www.nh-hotels.com

Hotel Madrid (€)

Built in 1910, and favoured by artists and intellectuals (General Franco stayed in room 3 in 1936), this friendly, family-run hotel is slowly being updated.

✉ Plaza de Cairasco 4 ☎ 928 36 06 64

Hotel Pujol (€)

Renovated budget hotel with access to the port and Playa de las Canteras.

✉ Calle Salvador Cuyas 5 ☎ 928 27 44 33

Hotel Reina Isabel (€€€)

A luxury hotel in a superb position on the Playa de las Canteras, with an excellent high-rise restauarnt, Parrilla Reina Isabel, and a gym and pool on the roof terrace.

✉ Calle Alfredo L Jones 40 ☎ 928 26 01 00; www.bullhotels.com

Hotel Residencia Majórica (€)

Right on Parque Santa Catalina and therefore likely to be noisy, but nonetheless is clean and cheap.

✉ Calle Ripoche 22 ☎ 928 26 28 78

Hotel Tryp Iberia (€€)

Very comfortable hotel in a good location right on the promenade with panoramic views to the sea. Facilities include a beauty centre.

✉ Avenida Alcalde José Ramírez Bethencourt 8 ☎ 928 36 11 33; www.solmelia.com

Marsin Playa (€€)

Comfortable apartments facing the beach at Las Canteras. It is worth paying the extra to get the sea views.

✉ Calle Luis Morote 54 ☎ 928 27 08 08

Meliá Las Palmas (€€)

Luxury hotel in the middle of Playa de las Canteras, with 312 rooms, shops, disco and a swimming pool.

✉ Calle Gomera 6 ☎ 928 26 80 50; www.solmelia.es

Sansofé Palace (€€€)

An excellent modern hotel, it occupies a fine position, near Playa de las Canteras. 115 rooms.

✉ Calle Portugal 68 ☎ 928 22 40 62; www.hotelesdunas.com

Santa Catalina (€€€)

Gran Canaria's top city hotel in a quiet, shady park. Canarian architecture, fine restaurant – Restaurante Doramas – and a casino. Tennis and squash courts, swimming pool. 208 rooms.

✉ León y Castillo 227, Parque Doramas ☎ 928 24 30 40; www.hotelsantacatalina.com

Verol (€–€€)

Good-value hotel located only a minute from the beach. The café/bar is popular.

✉ Calle Sagata ☎ 928 26 21 08

RESTAURANTS

Acueducto (€€–€€€)
A place for carnivores, with an array of meats grilled to your liking.
✉ Sargento Llagas 45 ☎ 928 26 42 42 🕐 Lunch, dinner

Amaiur (€€€)
One of the best eating places in the city specializes in the delicious subtly spicy tastes of Basque cuisine.
✉ Calle Perez Galdós 2 ☎ 928 37 07 17 🕐 Mon–Sat 1–4, 8:30–12

Ca'Cho Damian (€€)
If you're shopping in the Ballena mall, stop here for tasty *tapas* or a good meal of traditional Canarian fare.
✉ Centro Comercial La Ballena ☎ 928 41 73 00 🕐 All day

Café Madrid (€)
See page 60.

Café Regional Castilla-La Mancha (€€)
For a change from Canarian cooking head for this restaurant on the seafront, and enjoy hearty, meat-based cuisine from northern Spain – *jamón* (dry-cured ham) and *cochinillo* (roast suckling pig).
✉ Calle Nicolás Estévanez 80 (Paseo de Las Canteras) ☎ 928 22 90 82 🕐 Lunch, dinner

Café Vegueta (€€)
The popular evening bar-restaurant has good *tapas* and imaginative dishes of the day based on what's best from the nearby market.
✉ Calle Mendizábal 24 ☎ 928 33 13 21 🕐 Tue–Sun 4pm–2:30am

Canguro (€)
For the biggest croissants and cakes around, try this snack bar. A good place for breakfast before looking around Vegueta market.
✉ Calle Calvo Sotelo 1 ☎ 928 33 02 55 🕐 Open normal shopping hours

Casa Montesdeoca (€€€)
See page 60.

Don Quijote (€€)

Don't expect Spanish food in this Spanish-named restaurant. The flavour here is international, with the emphasis on steak.

✉ Calle Secretario Artiles 74 ☎ 928 27 27 86 🕔 Lunch, dinner

El Cid (€€–€€€)

Authentic Canarian cuisine not far from Playa de las Canteras. Local meats and fish a speciality.

✉ Calle Tomás Miller 73 ☎ 928 27 81 58 🕔 Lunch, dinner

El Cid Casa Pablo (€€€)

There's a wide choice of Basque and classic French dishes at this intimate restaurant. The wood-panelled interior is the perfect backdrop for grilled and roast meat, the house speciality, and you can enjoy tapas at the front bar.

✉ Calle Nicolás Estévanez 10 ☎ 928 22 46 31 🕔 Lunch, dinner

El Corte Inglés (€€€)

The popular lunchtime restaurant in this prestigious department store at the heart of town serves excellent food from an international menu.

✉ Avenida Mesa y Lopez 18 ☎ 928 26 30 00; www.elcorteingles.es
🕔 Lunch; closed Sun and hols

El Herreño (€–€€)

See page 58.

El Novillo Precoz (€€€)

A popular, family-run steak restaurant.

✉ Calle Portugal 9 ☎ 928 22 36 95 🕔 Tue–Sun lunch, dinner

El Padrino (€€)

Above the Puerto de la Luz in Las Coloradas, this popular restaurant serves excellent fish and seafood dishes, as well as Canarian classics.

✉ Calle Jesús Nazareno 1 ☎ 928 46 85 72 🕔 Lunch, dinner

El Pote (€€€)
Galician food and wine is the speciality here, although Canarian dishes like potatoes in *mojo* sauce and rabbit stew are excellent.
✉ Pasaje Juan Manuel Durán 41 ☎ 928 27 80 58 🕓 Lunch, dinner; Sun lunch only

Hipócrates (€€)
See page 61.

Julio (€€€)
A restaurant decorated in nautical style; naturally, offers fish and seafood as its speciality.
✉ Calle La Naval 132 ☎ 928 46 01 39 🕓 Mon–Sat lunch, dinner

La Casita (€€€)
On the edge of Parque Doramas, with two dining rooms and a covered terrace, caters for a discerning clientele.
✉ Calle León y Castillo 227 ☎ 928 24 54 64 🕓 Lunch, dinner

La Marinera (€€–€€€)
Restaurant with wonderful panoramic views of the bay, serves grills with meats from Uruguay and Argentina. Good fish, too.
✉ Paseo de las Canteras, C/Alonso Ojeda ☎ 928 46 88 02; www.lamarineraycasacarmelo.com 🕓 Daily 12:30–midnight

La Pasta Real (€€)
Italian cooking, excellent pasta and good vegetarian dishes.
✉ Calle Secretario Padilla 28 ☎ 928 26 22 67 🕓 Wed–Mon lunch, dinner

Rías Bajas (€€€)
A popular but pricey restaurant serving Galician-style seafood.
✉ Calle Simón Bolívar 5 ☎ 928 27 13 16 🕓 Lunch, dinner

Sakura (€€€)
Local fish is used to full effect at this Japanese restaurant, which offers a splendid range of sushi and sashimi, tempura and noodles.
✉ Calle Pilarillo Seco 5 ☎ 928 36 26 49 🕓 Lunch, dinner

SHOPPING

BOOKS
La Librería
See page 77.

DEPARTMENT STORES
El Corte Inglés
See page 76.

Hipercor
You'll need your own transport to take full advantage of this massive department store/shopping centre, where you'll find everything from food and drink to electrical and electronic goods, games, toys, perfumes and stationery. Prices are excellent.
✉ Avenida Pintor Felo Monzón s/n ☎ 928 42 30 00

Marks & Spencer
Las Palmas' main branch of the international store.
✉ Avenida Mesa y Lopez 32 ☎ 928 26 35 83

ELECTRONIC GOODS
Maya
A reputable chain of selling cameras, videos, TVs, mobile phones, software and a multitude of other electrical goods. Also sunglasses and jewellery.
✉ Calle Mayor de Triana 107 ☎ 928 37 12 55 ✉ Buenos Aires 4 ☎ 928 36 93 91

FASHION
Boutique Gema
Modern clothes for young women.
✉ Calle Travieso 13 ☎ 928 36 27 79

Boutique Ibio
Smart Canarios, both ladies and gentlemen, favour this fashion store, particularly for Gucci accessories.
✉ Calle Viera y Clavijo 6 ☎ 928 36 09 80

Boutique Marco Polo

Indian silks, pashminas, saris, Spanish shawls, flamenco dresses.

✉ Calle Sagastas 44 ☎ 928 27 42 10

Zara

High fashion geared to young tastes. Also at León y Castillo 27
(☎ 928 84 44 92).

✉ Calle Mayor de Triana 39 ☎ 928 38 27 32

FOOD AND DRINK

Cumbres Canarías

This deli stocks sausages and cheeses from all parts of the island,
as well as snacks and sandwiches to take away.

✉ Tomás Miller 47–49 ☎ 928 47 22 46

Morales

A traditional *pasteleria* selling delicious cakes and pastries.

✉ Calle Viera y Clavijo 4 ☎ 928 36 06 35

HANDICRAFTS

FEDAC

See page 72.

Higmara

See page 72.

Orbis

See page 73.

MARKETS

Mercado de Vegueta

See page 77.

Mercado del Puerto

Popular with sailors from ships docked in port. Like most Canarian
markets, it stays open 7am until 2pm.

✉ Calle Albareda

Mercado de las Flores

Arts, crafts and flower market held on Sunday mornings in the attractive old city square.

✉ Plaza de Santo Domingo

PERFUMES

Arkay

You'll find a wide range of top-name cosmetics and perfumes at this helpful store.

✉ Calle Luis Morote 22 ☎ 928 27 04 19

Defa

Offers a good selection of cosmetics and perfumes. All the major brands are here.

✉ Calle Galicia 27. There are several other branches in the city, including at Calle Cano 4 and Calle Tajaraste 4 ☎ 928 26 82 18

Yves Rocher

Huge range of perfumes and beauty goods at reasonable prices.

✉ Calle Nestor de la Torre 36 ☎ 928 24 73 89

TOBACCO

Juan Marquez

See page 72.

ENTERTAINMENT

FILMS

The International Film Festival of Las Palmas de Gran Canaria has been running since 1999 and is held in March in the Alfredo Kraus Auditorium (➤ 102) – for exact dates contact the tourist office – and has as many as 14 countries competing for a range of awards for 'best of', for example, directors, short films and photography.

Multicines La Ballena

Based in the shopping/entertainment complex by the southern exit out of town. Mostly foreign and dubbed mainstream films.

✉ La Ballena Centro Comercial ☎ 902 33 22 11

Multicines Las Arenas
Located in Las Arenas shopping mall, at the west end of Las Canteras beach.
✉ Carretera del Rincón s/n ☎ 928 26 16 00

Multicines Monopol
Another option in the Galeria de Arte Monopo, in the student quarter of the old town.
✉ Plaza de Mendoza s/n ☎ 928 36 74 38

Multicines Royal
A choice of screens and mainstream films.
✉ Calle León y Castillo 40 ☎ 928 36 09 54

Warner
Located in the El Muelle shopping centre near the port, this is a good venue to see the latest releases.
✉ El Muelle de Santa Catalina s/n ☎ No phone; see local newspapers for information

THEATRE AND CONCERTS
Auditorio Alfredo Kraus
A major venue for classical music concerts and a conference centre right on the beach with great sea views.
✉ Avenida Príncipe de Asturias ☎ 928 49 17 70; www.auditorio-alfredokraus.com ④ Ticket office: Mon–Fri,10–2, 4:30–8:30, Sat 10–2

Teatro Cuyás
This theatre opened in 2000 in a former cinema in Triana and hosts a range of productions from drama, comedy and ballet.
✉ Calle Viera y Clavijo s/n ☎ 928 43 21 80; www.teatrocuyas.com 🚌 1

Teatro Pérez Galdós
Home to the island's symphony orchestra and operatic society, the theatre hosts visits from international performers. Closed for extensive restoration, the theatre reopened in 2008.
✉ Plaza de Stagno ☎ 928 36 15 09 🚌 1

The South

In the south – which, for the purposes of this guide, extends from Gando airport in the east to Puerto de la Aldea in the west – the sun shines almost constantly and, despite the attractions of Las Palmas and the growth of inland tourism, the vast majority of visitors to Gran Canaria stay on the south coast. As a result the great resorts, many catering to mass tourism, are clustered here, including San Agustín, Playa del Inglés, Maspalomas and Puerto Rico.

At first sight they look like brash, concrete cities in a barren landscape. Then, little by little, their appeal becomes clear: Playa del Inglés, divided from Maspalomas by spectacular sand dunes; Puerto Rico, lively and friendly; Puerto de Mogán, beautifully planned and calmer; Playa de Taurito, dramatic and floral.

The interior is barely 20 minutes' drive from any coastal point. Ridges of cindery, volcanic rock separate deep ravines. White villages provide oases of palms and olives, and, in springtime, a plenitude of almond blossom.

Once discovered, this region is never forgotten.

□ Playa des Inglés

AGÜÍMES

In the east of the island, at the mouth of the Barranco de Guayadeque, is the town of Agüímes, surrounded by terraced hills. This administrative centre of an area famous for fruit and vegetables was once, from 1483 to 1811, the seat of the bishops of Gran Canaria, and its citizens enjoyed privileges not extended to the rest of the island.

The imposing neoclassical church of San Sebastián is testimony to the town's early importance. A small square just above the church, surrounded by dark ficus trees, is a pleasant spot for various civic events and festivities and the lively carnival in February.

The area surrounding Agüímes, dotted with caves and cave dwellings, supported an extensive population in pre-Hispanic times. Today the town is renowned for its team of Canarian wrestlers, Unión Agüímes. Canarian wrestling – *lucha canaria* – is a competition between two teams of wrestlers dressed in T-shirts and shorts, and fought in a sand-covered ring. This is one of several sports in Gran Canaria with direct roots in Guanche tradition.

✚ 22H ✉ Municipality of Agüímes: 30km (19 miles) south of Las Palmas, 28km (17 miles) northeast of Playa del Inglés 🍴 Bars and cafés in the square (€) 🚌 11, 21 from Las Palmas; 41, 52 from Maspalomas ❓ Thursday market. Feast of the Rosary, 7 Oct

ARGUINEGUÍN

On an otherwise busy south coast, Arguineguín has for years been ignored by visitors – maybe due to the presence of a large cement factory on its outskirts. Now, hotels and apartments are being built for those who like the atmosphere of a lively little Canarian town. It has a good beach and, with an active fishing community, is famous for its fish restaurants. The highway extension means that the town does not suffer as much from traffic mayhem.

North of the town, Barranco de Arguineguín, a fertile gorge planted with papayas, passion fruit and avocadoes, rises from a flat valley floor towards the heights of the central mountains at Ayacata (► 143).

✚ 16M ✉ Municipality of Mogán: 66km (41 miles) southeast of Las Palmas, 14km (9 miles) west of Playa del Inglés ☎ 928 73 59 56 🍴 Cofradía de Pescadores (► 60), Avenida del Muelle, offers good fish meals (€€) 🚌 32 from Playa del Inglés 🛈 Tue and Thu market

ARINAGA

Arinaga is a fast-growing, low-rise town with a lighthouse, a dark, rocky foreshore and a pretty Paseo Marítimo. At one time the town used to make its living from tomatoes and fishing. Now, many of its citizens are recent immigrants from inland villages who work in tourism-related industries. The sand-and-pebble beach to the south of Arinaga is popular with dinghy sailors and windsurfers, while Bahía de Formas attracts different kinds of migrating birds. A new harbour is being constucted but is not yet finished. Meanwhile, there's extensive ongoing development between the main road and the town.

➕ 23J ✉ Municipality of Agüimes: 36km (22 miles) south of Las Palmas, 20km (12 miles) northeast of Playa del Inglés 🍴 Cafés in town (€–€€) 🚌 25, 52 from Maspalomas

BARRANCO DE GUAYADEQUE

Best places to see, ➤ 38–39.

CASTILLO DEL ROMERAL

This small, rather tatty, fishing village of low white houses is named after a castle which has long since disappeared. It is popular with those in search of simple but good fresh fish restaurants, many now in former fishermen's terraced cottages.

✚ 22L ✉ Municipality of San Bartolomé: 42km (26 miles) south of Las Palmas, 14km (9 miles) northeast of Playa del Inglés 🚌 52 from Maspalomas

DUNAS DE MASPALOMAS

Best places to see, ➤ 44–45.

INGENIO

Ingenio is a large, expanding town. Its name means 'sugarmill' recalling its early 16th-century role as a base for sugar production. The old town, spilling down narrow streets from the church of Our Lady of Candelaria, has some fine houses. Most visitors head for the northern suburb of Las Mejías and the **Museo de Piedras y Artesanía Canaria** (Museum of Rocks and Canarian Handicraft): it shows an indifferent collection of rocks but excellent handicraft, particularly the open threadwork *(calados)* and embroidery *(bordados)* for which Ingenio and the neighbouring village of Carrizal are known.

✚ 22H ✉ Municipality of Agüímes: 27km (17 miles) south of Las Palmas, 31km (19 miles) northeast of Playa del Inglés 🚌 11 from Las Palmas, 52 from Maspalomas

Museo de Piedras y Artesanía Canaria

✉ Camino Real de Gando 1 ☎ 928 78 12 24 🕐 Mon–Sat 8–6:30 🎟 Free 🍴 Small refreshment bar (€)

around the island

a drive

This drive takes you through Gran Canaria's most scenic landscape, with a chance to explore the precipitous west coast and experience the spectacular mountains and lush valleys of the interior.

From Playa del Inglés take the motorway (GC1) as far as Taurito, where it ends (26km/16miles).

En route you'll have the chance to detour down to the resorts that lie along the south coast.

Leave the motorway and take the GC200 up the barranco to Mogán (➤ 115). Continue up the valley, then follow the road west through increasingly mountainous terrain, before dropping down to San Nicolás (➤ 129) and its puerto, 7km/4 miles further on.

Through the town, the Mirador del Balcón yields magnificent cliff views, ushering in a thrilling corniche drive along the Andén Verde (➤ 36–37) to El Risco (10km/6miles). This road is not for the faint-hearted.

Just before Agaete (16 km/ 10 miles) turn left to Puerto de las Nieves (➤ 170).

This fishing and ferry port is dominated by the rock monolith beneath its cliffs known as El Dedo de Dios (Finger of God).

Continue through Agaete (➤ 160) and Guía (➤ 173) and along the north coast to take the

GC20 south towards Arucas (➤ 162–163) and continue on the GC43 to Teror (➤ 52–53; 28km/17 miles).

Allow time to visit these fascinating and beautiful towns, a world away in atmosphere from the southern resorts. From Teror follow the mountain roads to Tejeda (➤ 154), driving through some of the island's most dramatic landscape and passing the Cruz de Tejeda (➤ 144) along the way (18km/ 12 miles). From Tejeda you'll start to lose height, as the GC60 starts its descent towards San Bartolomé de Tirajana (➤ 152). Continue through the town south on the GC60, passing the village of Fataga (➤ 147), until you emerge from the mountains and see the south coast lying ahead. The GC60 leads directly through San Fernando into Playa del Inglés

Distance Approximately 165km (100 miles)
Time 6 hours' driving, but allow all day
Start/end point Playa del Inglés ✚ 19M
Lunch El Dedo de Dios (€€€; ➤ 181) ⊠ Puerto de las Nieves

JUAN GRANDE

This small complex of church, manorial home and garden/palm grove belongs to the De Vega Grande family. The family's extensive estates consisted mostly of dry land, good only for growing tomatoes. But in the late 1950s, Don Alejandro del Castillo, Conde de la Vega Grande, launched the first tourist development in southern Gran Canaria at San Agustín. By the 1970s the San Agustín/Playa del Inglés/Maspalomas resort

was firmly on the tourist map and Gran Canaria had become a year-round holiday destination for northern Europeans. Tourism now accounts for 80 per cent of the gross national product of the island.

✚ 21L ✉ Municipality of San Bartolomé de Tirajana: 40km (25 miles) south of Las Palmas, 12km (7 miles) northeast of Playa del Inglés
🍴 Fish restaurants in nearby Castillo del Romeral (€) 🚌 30, 44, 60, 90 from Maspalomas; 1 from Las Palmas

LOMO DE LOS LETREROS

The 'Ridge of the Inscriptions', in the Barranco de Balos, is a remarkable aboriginal site: a rock face, 300m (327yds) long, bearing incised sketches of the human form, and geometric patterns such as concentric circles, spirals and triangles. Much weathered over the years, it has also been considerably defaced. The etched shape of something resembling a boat is significant in view of the fact that, by the time they were conquered, the islanders had lost all knowledge of navigation and boating. Local environmentalists disapprove of open access. As with many of Gran Canaria's important archaeological sites, lack of funding and official neglect compound the problems created by graffiti-writers and souvenir-hunters. The site is closed to the public at the time of writing, but it is posssible it may reopen in the future.

✚ 21H ✉ Municipality of Santa Lucía de Tirajana: 33km (20 miles) south of Las Palmas, 23km (14 miles) northeast of Playa del Inglés 🍴 Cafés in nearby Cruce de Sardina (€–€€€)

ℹ Agüimes tourist office ☎ 928 12 41 83

MASPALOMAS

Although the twin resorts of Maspalomas and Playa del Inglés
(► 122–123) have virtually merged into a single tourist
conurbation, Maspalomas still has a more up-market image, no
doubt due to its magnificent dunes (► 44–45) and the early
building of luxury hotels around the oasis.

The lighthouse *(faro)* and the bus and taxi terminus mark the
western boundary of the resort. From here a promenade runs
past chic shopping centres, bars and restaurants and ends at the
Barranco de Maspalomas, which, at this seaward point, is
occupied by a fenced-off lagoon *(charco)* with reed beds, pampas
grass and resident and migratory birds. The Sardinian warbler
nests in this area amid the tamarisk groves between February
and June.

Environmentalists are making themselves heard in the debate
between developers and conservationists, particularly in relation
to the dunes and the lagoon, and there is an Information and
Interpretation Centre behind the Hotel Riu Palace in Playa del
Inglés. Beach and dunes stretch east from here to join the sands
at Playa del Inglés.

To the west of the lighthouse, the neighbouring upscale resort of Las Meloneras has a sheltered bay, shopping mall, and a luxury hotel designed in traditional Canarian style.

North of the lagoon, the *barranco* turns into a dry river course with the prestigious 18-hole Maspalomas Campo de Golf to one side. Estates of select apartments give way to denser holiday accommodation, skirted by wide avenues named after tour operators like Tui, Thomson and Neckermann. The Faro 2 *centro comercial* is a circular complex of shops, bars and restaurants. Amusement parks mark the resort's northern edge.

✚ 18M ✉ Municipality of San Bartolomé de Tirajana: 30km (19 miles) southwest of Las Palmas, 6km (4 miles) southwest of Playa del Inglés

🍴 Cafés everywhere (€–€€€) 🚌 Frequent service from Playa del Inglés including 1, 30; 30 from Las Palmas

WHAT TO SEE AROUND MASPALOMAS
Aqualand

This water park, the biggest in the Canary Islands, is situated in the Barranco de Chamoriscán, north of Maspalomas. Ideal for a family day out, it offers 29 slides, a slow river, wave pool, children's pools, a self-service café and large car park. The entry price covers unlimited use of all the park's attractions.

www.aqualand.es

✚ 18L ✉ Mte León, Carretera Palmitos Parque km3, Maspalomas ☎ 928 14 05 25 🕐 Summer daily 10–6; winter daily 10–5 ✋ Moderate 🍴 On premises (€) 🚌 45, 70 from Maspalomas

Camel Safari Park

La Barranda Camel Safari Park is 12km (7.5 miles) north from Playa del Inglés on the road toward Fataga This palm-planted oasis is home to a herd of camels who take visitors on half-hour tours of the valley, with a chance for kids to get right up close to the animals. Riders sit in seats suspended from the camels, and the experience is followed by lunch.

✉ La Barranda, Ruta de Fataga ☎ 928 79 86 80 ⏰ Daily 10–5:30 🎟 Moderate 🍴 Café and restaurant on site (€) ❓ Buses pick up pre-booked guests from hotels. Camel shows on Tue, Thu and Sat at 3pm

Holiday World

Holiday World has something for all those who want a noisy, fun time. All the fun of the fair, with rollercoaster, dodgems and roundabouts, plus bars, restaurants, bowling lanes, gym, two big discos and amusement arcades.

✉ Carretera General Las Palmas ☎ 928 73 34 98 ⏰ Sun–Thu 9–2, Fri–Sat 9–6 🚌 45, 70 from Maspalomas

Perla Canaria

On the road to Palmitos Park, next to Aqualand, is a pearl factory – exhibition centre, workshop and gem store. You can watch the craftsmen at work and pick a pearl to create your own jewellery. The showroom sells pearls, gold, semi-precious gems and gifts.

www.perlacanaria.com

✉ Carretera a Palmitos Park ☎ 928 14 14 64 ⏰ Daily 9–7.30 🍴 Tropical tea garden on premises (€) 🚌 45, 70 from Maspalomas

MOGÁN

Mogán lies some 10km (6 miles) inland from the sea and its own harbour, Puerto de Mogán. The *barranco* running between the two is rich with tropical fruits; the slowly climbing road is lined almost continuously with hamlets. Numerous houses here are built in traditional rustic style, with large stones emerging through white rendering to create an attractive piebald effect. The little white town itself is comfortable and of some importance: it is from here that the whole district, including the coastline from Arguineguín to Puerto de Mogán and even further west, is governed.

✚ 15J ✉ Municipality of Mogán: 88km (55 miles) southwest of Las Palmas, 37km (23 miles) northwest of Playa del Inglés 🍴 Cafés in town (€–€€€)
🚌 84 from Puerto de Mogán, 86 from Maspalomas

MUNDO ABORIGEN

Mundo Aborigen (► 68) is based on the chronicles of the first invaders, who found the aboriginal people living in well-organized, close-knit groups. They are described as gentle and kindly, lovers of sport and music and redoubtable in battle. The spirit of the Guanches is strongly evoked in the beauty of the hillside and the views from here. To the west, dark striated gorges recede into the distance, and to the south, at the mouth of the *barranco*, lies the city of Playa del Inglés and the Maspalomas dunes.

✚ 19K ✉ Carretera de Fataga ☎ 928 17 22 95 🕙 Daily 9–6 📶 Moderate
🍴 Café and souvenir shop on premises (€€) 🚌 18 from Maspalomas

PALMITOS PARQUE

Spread over a huge area at the head of the Barranco de Chamoriscán, this park is one of the island's principal attractions. Exotic birds – 230 different species, many of them uncaged – include flamingoes, toucans, cranes, macaws, hornbills, peacocks and tiny hummingbirds.

The park opened in the 1970s and has been regularly extended and improved. An aquarium in a dramatic natural setting, with vast concave glass tanks set in rock surrounds, provides a panoramic view. Tropical fish from the Pacific region and the Amazon can be seen here.

Winding paths lead from one point of interest to another past a stream, a palm grove (there are 51 varieties among the 1,000 palms), clumps of giant euphorbia, to a small island, home to a couple of white gibbons. The heated butterfly house has butterflies from all over the world, and the orchid house, said to be the first in Spain, is also spectacular. There are plenty of shady benches and cafés.

A favourite with children is the parrot show, included in the entry fee. A well-trained troupe of macaws walks tightropes and rides bicycles to enthusiastic applause. Exciting birds of prey shows attract a large crowd.

In 2007, a catastrophic fire swept across the south of Gran Canaria, destroying much of the park area. All the animals were safely evacuated and it's hoped things willl be back to normal in the near future.

➕ 18K ✉ Barranco de Chamoriscán: 55km (34 miles) southwest of Las Palmas, 15km (9 miles) northwest of Playa del Inglés ☎ 928 14 02 76
🕐 Daily 10–6 ✋ Expensive 🍴 Cafés and souvenir shops in park (€€)
🚌 Free bus services from Playa del Inglés, San Agustín and Puerto Rico
❓ Parrot shows every hour from 11am. Birds of prey shows at 12:30 and 3:30

PASITO BLANCO

This attractive complex of houses, yacht club and marina lies in a sheltered bay just west of Maspalomas. Though it is private, the public may walk down from the GC500 highway into the resort to swim off the small beach to the right of the jetty, or dive off the rocks into Pasito Blanco's famously clear waters. Fifteen minutes' walk along the track to the west brings you to Playa de las Mujeres, where nude bathing is common and people occasionally camp out (illegally) at night. Another 30-minute walk brings you to the Playa de la Arena (no shops or beach bars on the way).

A track in the opposite direction from Pasito Blanco, towards Maspalomas, brings you first to a fine sandy beach, Playa del Hornillo, and then to Las Meloneras, a wide, curved beach with a growing tourist development. This is dominated by the Lopesan Costa Meloneras Hotel, home to a super-luxury spa. Around it a shopping mall, golf course and casino have sprung up, attracting wealthy visitors. The shining globe in the arid hills above Pasito Blanco, visible from the road, is the NASA space tracking station, the Estación de Seguimiento Espacial de Maspalomas.

✚ 18M ✉ Municipality of San Bartolomé: 57km (35 miles) southwest of Las Palmas, 5km (3 miles) west of Playa del Inglés 🍴 Restaurant in camping site behind marina at Pasito Blanco (€) 🚌 91 from Las Palmas and Playa del Inglés/Maspalomas

PATALAVACA

Patalavaca, literally 'Cow's Foot', is reputed to have the longest hours of sunshine on the island; it also offers a beach of light-coloured sand and flat rocks. Not surprisingly, this small resort is dense with steeply rising hotels and apartment blocks. The clientele is mostly Scandinavian. A coastal walkway connects Patalavaca with its neighbour, Arguineguín (► 105).

✚ 16L ✉ Municipality of San Bartolomé de Tirajana: 68km (42 miles) southwest of Las Palmas, 16km (10 miles) west of Playa del Inglés
🚌 91 (as above)

a walk to Playa del Inglés

This walk follows the coastal promenade from San Agustín (➤ 128–129) to Playa del Inglés (➤ 122), and continues along the beach, around the Maspalomas dunes, to end at Maspalomas lighthouse. There is no shade on the beach; walk early morning or late evening and take plenty of water.

Start from the grey-sand beach at San Agustín, taking the much improved promenade to the right, past hotel gardens at first, then apartments.

Climbing a little above rocks, the path circles round to the beach of Las Burras, where a few fishing boats rest on the sands. The hotels of Playa del Inglés are now firmly in view.

Along the promenade, continue ahead to cross the wooden footbridge.

The bar on the right-hand side of the bridge, Kioska Las Burras, serve tasty *bocadillos* (bread rolls with a filling), salad and beer, plus wonderful freshly squeezed fruit drinks.

Passing the Europalace Hotel, the promenade ascends several flights of steps to follow the top of a modest cliff. At the centre of Playa del Inglés, it descends again to cross the only road along the route (Avenida de Alfereces Provisionales). Turn left along the road on to the beach, by now golden in colour, then follow the beach to the right.

Narrow at first, it soon expands into a wide wedge, with beach beds and beach bars and, towards the end, a nudist zone. Behind, the golden dunes now rise, not in long ridges but in individual hillocks.

Follow the fringe of beach around the dunes. Twenty minutes from the corner brings you to Maspalomas. Pass the freshwater pond to the right, then keep to the sea for the lighthouse.

Distance 8km (5 miles)
Time 2.5 hours
Start point San Agustín ✚ 20L
End point Maspalomas ✚ 18M
Lunch El Señador beach bar (€), before the lighthouse

PLAYA DEL INGLÉS

The first-time visitor to Playa del Inglés is likely to get lost among identical streets with identical hotels. There is no obvious town centre, no charming plaza with trees and outdoor cafés. Most of the life, apart from that of beach and hotel, is concentrated on commercial centres *(centros comerciales)* containing hundreds of small shops, bars, restaurants and entertainments. They are worth visiting only in the evening.

On the plus side, sunshine is almost guaranteed, the beach is splendid and the resort has accommodation in every category; restaurants to suit every palate and purse; and is well-served with buses, taxis and car-rental agencies and even a miniature train.

The nearest thing to a town centre is the vast complex of the Yumbo Centrum, with the main Tourist Information Office on Avenida de Estados Unidos. The Yumbo, the largest of about 11 such centres in Playa del Inglés alone is a vast bazaar of inexpensive goods. Of the many bars, restaurants and entertainments on offer, a substantial number caters for the gay community. The focus of young nightlife revolves around the *centros comerciales* like the Kasbah or the Metro grouped around the Ecumenical Church of San Salvador, on Calle de Malaga. Cita Centre is also popular.

In the early evening, the heart of Playa del Inglés is the coastal promenade, the Paseo Costa Canario, which runs along the coast from San Agustín (➤ 128–129) to Maspalomas (➤ 112–113).

The northern district of San Fernando is home to Canarian workers in the tourist industry. It provides the chance of eating in local *tapas* bars and restaurants at local prices, and of stocking up on groceries at prices lower than in the resorts. There is also a wrestling stadium beside the football ground.

✚ 19M ✉ Municipality of San Bartolomé de Tirajana: 52km (32 miles) south of Las Palmas 🚌 30 from Las Palmas; numerous local buses
🛈 Yumbo Centrum ☎ 928 76 41 96

PUERTO DE LA ALDEA

The little harbour town of Puerto de la Aldea, sheltering under a mountainous cape to the north, was long the only practical means of reaching San Nicolás de Tolentino (➤ 129), just inland. The *puerto* has a small selection of fish restaurants and a promenade, with distant views of Tenerife, leading south along the rocky beach. Behind, among pine trees, is an extensive *merendero* (picnic area), with tables and seating. Beyond, in the *barranco* bed, lies a freshwater pond, or *charco* – the finishing point of the famous *Fiesta del Charco* (Festival of the Lagoon), which takes place 7–11 September. In a ceremony of pre-Hispanic origin, local people would bring down palm branches and beat the water with

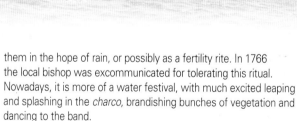

them in the hope of rain, or possibly as a fertility rite. In 1766 the local bishop was excommunicated for tolerating this ritual. Nowadays, it is more of a water festival, with much excited leaping and splashing in the *charco*, brandishing bunches of vegetation and dancing to the band.

✚ 1E ✉ Municipality of San Nicolás de Tolentino: 76km (47 miles) southwest of Las Palmas, 75km (46 miles) northwest of Playa del Inglés 🍴 Good fish restaurants in town (€–€€€) 🚌 38 from Puerto de Mogán, 101 from Gáldar

PUERTO DE MOGÁN

Best places to see, ➤ 50–51.

PUERTO RICO

They say there will be no new building in this brash resort because there is no room left – not for the tiniest hotel or even apartment.

Puerto Rico grew up on the strength of its constant sunshine and the protection of encircling hills. The wide, man-made beach (with sand from the Sahara desert) shelves gently into the sea, making this a popular destination for families with small children. The western arm of the beach turns into a port, busy with offers of deep-sea-fishing, sailing, diving, windsurfing, jet-skiing and parascending trips. In fact Puerto Rico is one of the world capitals of big game fishing. More than 30 world records have been set here. Among the fish that swim in the waters off the south coast of Gran Canaria are albacora, big-eye, yellowfin and skipjack tuna, bonito, barracuda, swordfish, shark and wahoo, but the ultimate prize is the blue marlin, which can weigh anything between 250 and 500kg (550–1,100 lbs). To see a blue marlin being caught is to witness an epic sporting battle between man and beast which you are never quite sure who is going to win. The best time to hunt for marlin is between May and October, while tuna are mostly caught during the winter. Boats offer daily fishing trips all the year from the two harbours.

Another man-made beach, the fast-developing Playa de los Amadores, can be reached in around 20 minutes, by a clifftop path to the west.

Puerto Rico has a rarity among southern resorts: a town park, planted with ficus trees and palms, behind the beach. There is also a heated swimming pool, a bowling-alley, floodlit tennis, *fronton* (the Spanish alternative to 'fives') and mini-golf courts, a water park and a *centro comercial* full of inexpensive shops and fast-food restaurants.

✠ 16L ✉ Municipality of Mogán: 72km (45 miles) southwest of Las Palmas, 20km (12 miles) west of Playa del Inglés 🍴 Choice of beach and town restaurants (€–€€€) 🚌 1, 91 from Las Palmas, 32 from Playa del Inglés/Maspalomas

SAN AGUSTÍN

Southern Gran Canaria's first shovelful of tourist concrete was laid in San Agustín. Curiously, this resort, a step away from popular Playa del Inglés (➤ 122–123), has never been tarred with the brush of mass tourism. No doubt the presence of the 4-star Melia Tamarindos Hotel and its casino have helped to maintain its well-heeled image. It is a quieter and more sleepy resort with more of an appeal to older people, less emphasis on younger nightlife and more sophisticated restaurants.

The resort is cut in two by the GC500 highway, leaving the hillside half connected to the beachside half by a series of bridges. The main beach, the dark-sand Playa de San Agustín, has the small Playa del Morro Besudo to its east and Playa de las Burras to the west. The three large hotels (including the Tamarindos), all in Calle de las Retamas, are known for their splendid gardens. Much of the other accommodation is in low-rise apartments. San Agustín has its share of good restaurants, but none are in the *centro comercial*.

A short distance northeast of San Agustín, at a suitably noisy juncture between the *carretera* and the motorway, is the **Gran Karting Club** (➤ 64). Its 1,200m (1,308yds) of track for go-carts and mini-carts is the longest in Spain and its clientele is of all ages and even caters for the under fives. There is a pleasant lounge, café and games room and a sunny terrace for spectators.

✚ 20L ✉ Municipality of San Bartolomé de Tirajana: 48km (30 miles) southwest of Las Palmas, 4km (2.5 miles) northeast of Playa del Inglés

Gran Karting Club

✉ Carretera General del Sur km 46 ☎ 928 15 71 90 ⏰ Summer daily 11–10; winter daily 10–9 💷 Moderate 🍴 Café (€)

SAN NICOLÁS DE TOLENTINO

Sometimes known as 'La Aldea' or 'The Village', San Nicolás de Tolentino is tomato town. In a broad and dusty valley, plastic greenhouses spread out in all directions. Towards the end of the season, tomato surpluses are dumped on wasteground, making brilliant splashes of colour. The town itself is mostly residential, with a cluster of shops round the church square and its restored Canarian-style church. Near by, in Tocodoman, is the excellent **Cactualdea Park** with impressive cactus plants and exhibitions.

✚ 2E ✉ Municipality of San Nicolás de Tolentino: 71km (44 miles) southwest of Las Palmas, 70km (43 miles) northwest of Playa del Inglés 🍴 Cafés in town (€–€€€) 🚌 38 from Puerto de Mogán

Cactualdea Park

✉ Tocodoman ☎ 928 78 90 57; www.cactualdea.info ⏰ Daily 10–6 💷 Moderate

SIOUX CITY

In the dry Barranco de Aguila, northwest of San Agustín and 300m (330yds) from the beach, Sioux City is a Wild West theme park that has been created in the remains of an old spaghetti-western-style film set. Contributing towards the one-horse-town atmosphere are re-created saloons, church, bank, prison, bar and a sheriff's office. An action-packed show includes such diversions as knife-throwing, lassooing, pistol-shooting and, naturally enough, a bank robbery.

✚ 20L ✉ Cañón del Aguila ☎ 928 76 25 73 🕐 Tue–Sun 10–5 ✋ Moderate 🍴 Cafés on premises (€€) 🚌 29 from Maspalomas ❓ Shows 12, 1:30, 3, 4:30

VECINDARIO

Vecindario is a workaday town which stretches interminably along the main coast road. It is a modern creation born of rural depopulation and the demands of the tourist industry. Once a small village in a tomato-growing area, its size and relative prosperity have earned it the label *la ciudad de los Mercedes* – 'Mercedes city'. Street markets in Plaza San Rafael and Era de Verdugo sell excellent local produce. The town is home to the Centro Comercial Atlántico, the biggest mall easily accessible from the southern resorts.

✚ 22K ✉ Municipality of Santa Lucía de Tirajana: 18km (11 miles) northeast of Playa del Inglés 🍴 Many cafés (€–€€€)

HOTELS

ARGUINEGUÍN
Anfi del Mar (€€)
See page 70.

Hotel Dunas La Canaria (€€€)
See page 70.

MASPALOMAS/PLAYA DEL INGLÉS/SAN AGUSTÍN
Gloria Palace (€€)
Large, well-established hotel in San Agustín with a new thalassotherapy (sea-water therapy) centre adjacent which is open to non-residents.
✉ Las Margaritas, San Augustín ☎ 928 12 85 00 (hotel), 928 77 64 04 (thalassotherapy centre); www.hotelgloriapalace.com

Grand Hotel Residencia (€€€)
This designer hotel is fast becoming one of the most exclusive on the island, with attractive rooms in villas set around a pool.
✉ Avenida del Oasis 32, Maspalomas ☎ 928 72 31 00; www.grand-hotel-residencia.com

Iberostar Costa Canaria (€€€)
A beautiful hotel set in verdant tropical gardens beside the sea. All rooms have balconies with sea views, breakfast and lunch are served outside on the terrace and there are three pools, with reserved sunbeds for guests.
✉ Las Retamas 1, San Agustín ☎ 928 76 02 00; wwwiberostar.com

IFA Faro Maspalomas (€€€)
See page 71.

Meliá Tamarindos (€€€)
Luxury hotel in a quiet situation with superb gardens; casino and cabaret on premises.
✉ Las Retamas 3, San Agustín ☎ 928 77 40 90

Palacio Dunamar (€€€)
See page 71.

Riu Grand Palace Maspalomas Oasis (€€€)
See page 71.

PUERTO DE MOGÁN
Hotel Taurito Princess (€€€)
See page 70.

SAN NICOLÁS DE TOLENTINO
Hotel Los Cascajos (€)
Simple accommodation with 20 rooms and a restaurant.
✉ C/Los Cascajos 9 ☎ 928 89 11 65

RESTAURANTS

AGÜIMES
La Tartería (€)
In the town's old square, this is a pleasant place for a snack with good home-made cakes and pies. There is a good choice of coffees and ice-creams. Welcoming, with friendly service.
✉ Plaza del Rosario 21 ☎ 928 78 77 38 🕐 Lunch, dinner

Tagoror (€€)
See page 59.

ARGUINEGUÍN
Bahía (€€)
Overlooking the harbour, this friendly restaurant serves tourists and locals alike with excellent fresh fish dishes.
✉ Avenida Del Muelle 6 ☎ 928 73 53 81 🕐 10:30–10:30

Cofradía de Pescadores (€€)
See page 60.

MASPALOMAS/PLAYA DEL INGLÉS/SAN AGUSTÍN

Amaiur (€€€)
See page 58.

Chipi-Chipi (€€)
See page 60.

Gorbea (€€€)
See page 59.

Guatiboa (€€€)
See page 59.

El Duomo di Milano (€€)
This restaurant serves excellent Italian and Mediterranean dishes.
✉ Calle Hannover 4, Playa del Inglés ☎ 928 76 37 95 ⏱ 12–4, 7–12

El Senador (€€)
Right by the lighthouse on Mapalomas beach, this relaxed
restaurant even has its own sunbathing terrace. The menu
includes fish, shellfish and simple roast meats, but try the paella,
accompanied by the house sangria. Reservations recommended.
✉ Paseo del Faro, Maspalomas ☎ 928 14 04 96 ⏱ Lunch, dinner

Greek Taverna (€€)
This authentic restaurant imports its essential ingredients direct
from Greece, serving up Greek salad with feta, *dolmades* and
moussaka. Try a selection from the huge range of *mezes*.
✉ Local 67–69, Centro Comercial San Agustín, San Agustín ☎ 928 76 67 85
⏱ Lunch, dinner

La Casa Vieja (€–€€)
This is, in fact, two restaurants on either side of the road. On
the left as you come up the hill is the more traditional, serving
chargrilled meats. On the right, El Rincón, the more expensive
option, specializes in fish. Book ahead for a table in the garden.
✉ El Lomo, Carrtera a Fataga ☎ 928 76 99 18 ⏱ Lunch, dinner

La Toja (€€€)
See page 59.

Las Camelias (€)
Probably the best of the many buffet restaurants in Playa del Inglés, providing a huge self-service selection that includes a salad bar, seafood, Canarian dishes, roasts and freshly barbecued steaks and chicken. Exceptional value for money.

✉ Avenida de Tirajana 15, Playa del Inglés ☎ 928 76 02 36 🕔 Lunch, dinner

Las Cumbres Canarias (€€)
This typically Spanish restaurant in Playa del Inglés serves excellent roast lamb.

✉ Avenida de Tirajana 9, Playa del Inglés ☎ 928 76 09 41 🕔 Lunch, dinner

Loopy's (€€)
Grilled meat and pizzas and a lively atmosphere in a Swiss-chalet-type restaurant.

✉ Las Retamas 7, San Agustín ☎ 928 76 28 92 🕔 Lunch, dinner

Los Pescadores (€)
It is only due to the high level of tourism that this restaurant includes pizzas on its menu. Well-known for its typically Canarian dishes, it serves mainly fish, plus a good selection of grilled meats.

✉ Bahía Feliz, San Agustín ☎ 928 15 71 79 🕔 Lunch, dinner

Marieta Buffet Grill (€–€€)
One of many self-service restaurants – it's good value, has huge selections, and you can eat all you want.

✉ Avenida Italia 15, Playa del Inglés ☎ 928 77 34 14 🕔 Breakfast, lunch, dinner

MOGÁN
Cofradía de Pescadores (€€)
This fishermen's cooperative by the harbour serves good fresh grilled fish dishes. Try the warm bread served with garlic mayo.

✉ Dársena Exterior del Puerto ☎ 928 56 53 21 🕔 Lunch, dinner

Grill Acaymo (€€)

Rustic décor combined with thrilling terrace views. Canarian food a speciality here.

✉ El Tostador 14 ☎ 928 56 92 63 🕓 Tue–Sun 12–10:30; closed Sun evening

La Bodeguilla Juananá (€€)

Bar-restaurant plus deli selling local food and handicrafts.

✉ Puerto de Mogán ☎ 928 56 50 44 🕓 Dinner only

Patio Canario II (€€-€€€)

Specializing in fish, this attractive restaurant also serves grills and Canarian fare.

✉ Puerto de Mogán ☎ 928 56 52 74 🕓 Lunch, dinner

PUERTO RICO

Don Quijote (€€)

Serves international cuisine at low prices. There's a children's menu.

✉ Centro Comercial ☎ 928 56 09 01 🕓 Mon–Sat lunch, dinner

El Tiburón (€€)

With a name translated as 'the shark', this restaurant offers a range of fresh fish as well as a selection of excellent pizzas. You may be lured into the restaurant with offers of free *sangria*.

✉ Paseo Maritimo ☎ 928 56 05 57 🕓 Lunch, dinner

Gran Canaria (€€)

Not just barbecued meat and fish by the beach here. This restaurant serves huge steaks and a selection of great desserts – some complete with flaming sparklers. There is also live music.

✉ Playa de Puerto Rico ☎ 928 56 13 54 🕓 Lunch, dinner

Minanas Chillout (€€)

This classic Spanish restaurant prepares the best recipes from the different regions of mainland Spain. All ingredients are fresh, the prices are reasonable and the staff friendly.

✉ Castillo del Sol ☎ 928 56 03 34 🕓 Lunch, dinner

SHOPPING

ARQUINEGUÍN
Fish market
Held every morning. There is also a general market on Tuesday and Thursday.
✉ Arquineguín harbour

INGENIO
Museo de Piedras y Artesanía Canaria
See page 69.

MASPALOMAS
Faro 2
See page 76.

PLAYA DEL INGLÉS
Craft market
An evening craft market held in the Plaza de Maspalomas next to the mini-train. Good for presents.
✉ Plaza de Maspalomas ⏰ Mon–Sat 6–11

FEDAC
Canarian handicrafts sold at the Tourist Information Office. FEDAC's aim is to maintain and develop traditional crafts. The items on sale are guaranteed to be genuine Canarian craftsmanship. This helps to protect you and the seller from foreign replicas.
✉ Centro Insular de Turismo, Avenida de España (on corner with Avenida de los Estados Unidos) ☎ 928 77 24 45 ⏰ Mon–Fri 10–2, 4–7:30

La Galería
This shop is in the great warren of the Yumbo Centrum, the biggest commercial centre in Playa del Inglés. It stocks a range of island handicrafts, as well as various hand-crafted items from further afield. Worth a look for the occasional gems to be discovered here.
✉ Yumbo Centrum ☎ 928 76 41 96

Tienda FEDAC
See page 72.

Yumbo Centrum
See page 77.

PUERTO DE MOGÁN
Hijos de Sun
Stocks a wide selection of pure cotton and linen shirts, blouses and dresses; also embroidered jackets and coats from Japan.
✉ Edificio Arnel, Avenida de Artes, Puerto de Mogán ☎ 928 56 53 50

Fish market
This is another daily fish market. There is also a general market on Friday.
✉ Puerto de Mogán harbour 🕐 Daily 10–2

La Bodeguilla Juananá
See page 77.

Rincon Canario
This very stylishly decorated shop stocks a wide range of Canarian handicrafts – including ceramics, embroidery and basketwork.
✉ Puerto de Mogán, local 105 ☎ 928 56 40 44

SAN AGUSTÍN
Centro Comercial
A large commercial centre on three floors. These are huge shopping centres that also provide entertainment. There is a smaller one called El Pulpo.
✉ Calle de las Dalias

SAN FERNANDO
Market
A wide range of local goods on sale.
✉ Avenida Alejandro del Castillo s/n 🕐 Wed and Sat markets 8–2

San Fernando

Along with Botánico, the Mercado Municipal, Nilo and Eurocenter, this is an economical place to shop.

✉ Avenida de Tejeda, San Fernando

VECINDARIO
Centro Comercial Atlántico

See page 76.

Market

A variety of products sold on the weekly stalls.

✉ Avenida de Canarias, Vecindario ⏲ Wed 8–2

ENTERTAINMENT

Much of the entertainment in the south of the island is focused around hotels that have discos, karaoke evenings and flamenco nights. Tour operators will also be able to offer you a wide range of nights out.

Casino Tamarindos Palace

You have to be over 18, look respectable (that is, wear a jacket and a tie if you are male) and carry identification in order to gamble or even watch at this casino. There is also a caberet show.

✉ Hotel Tamarindos, C/Las Retamas 3, San Agustín

☎ 928 76 27 24

SPORT

DIVING

Gran Canaria is an ideal venue for scuba diving. As with most destinations, beginners will learn in swimming pools and sheltered harbours. However, for the more experienced, there is a lava reef off Pasito Blanco, where you can spot moray eels. For more information see www.gran-canaria-diving.com or www.canary-diving.com.

GOLF

There are eight excellent golf courses on the island, three on the south coast, and five on the north coast. It is realistically claimed that, thanks to the climate, you can play golf every day of the year.

PARASCENDING

Parascending, which involves flying up to 200m (660ft) in a parachute while attached to a boat, is available at Puerto Rico and Playa del Inglés. This is an expensive thrill, but like many of these activities, it is sometimes available at a discount when combined with a boat trip. Or try skydiving with an instructor (☎ 670 80 81 02; www.skydivegrancanaria.es).

WINDSURFING

Most beaches have equipment to rent and offer lessons to beginners and those wishing to improve their skills. Experienced windsurfers should head for Pozo Izquierdo on the southeast coast or Playa del Águila at San Agustín.

ARGUINEGUÍN
Dive Academy
See page 64.

Salobre Golf & Resort
Just off the the GC1 motorway near Arguineguín this golf course has fine views towards the sea and mountains. It is an 18-hole, par 71 course with additional driving range, putting green and restaurant.
✉ Urbanización El Salobre Golf ☎ 928 01 01 03; www.salobregolfresort.com

MASPALOMAS
Campo de Golf
See page 64.

PLAYA DEL INGLÉS
Canariaventura
See page 65.

Free Motion Biking
See page 65.

PUERTO DE MORGÁN
Atlantic Islands Sail Training Centre
See page 65.

PUERTO RICO
Aquanauts Dive Center
Run by a Finnish company which offers daily dives, night dives on Sun and Thu and full-day dives (two tanks) plus introductory courses for learners.
✉ Commercial Centre, Puerto Base, Local 5, Sotano
☎ 928 56 06 55; www.aquanauts-divecentre.com

Barakuda Dos
See page 64.

SAN AGUSTÍN
Dive Center Nautico
This German firm offers courses for beginners and takes more experienced divers out into deep water.
✉ IFA Club Atlantic, C/Los Jazmines 2
☎ 928 77 81 68

F2 Surfcenter Dunkerbeck
See page 65.

Central Gran Canaria

For those who love high mountains and volcanic landscapes, vast basalt columns rising solitary from rocky platforms, deep valleys, greenery, wild flowers in abundance – the centre has to be the place.

San Bartolomé
de Tirajana

Pico (Pozo) de las Nieves is the highest point, more a mountain rim than a peak, looking down over the southeast. The free-standing Roque Nublo, a vast trunk of stone, rises almost as high, and looks west and southwest. Mountain

villages, many with inhabited caves as well as houses, are gently domestic in atmosphere, white in colour, ancient in appearance. There are forests of Canarian pine, sometimes streaming with lichen, and echoing with woodpeckers. There are rocky hillsides dense with cistus, lavender, broom and thyme. There are short paths, long trails, rough roads and asphalt roads. Above all, there is a lofty landscape, offering drama and surprise at every turn.

ANDÉN VERDE

See pages 36–37.

ARTEARA

Most visitors become aware of this
tiny, fertile village, set in the
beautiful Barranco de Fataga, only
when they come here on camel
safari. The camel ride skirts the
village and by-passes one of the
most interesting pre-Hispanic sites
on the island: an ancient necropolis,
containing hundreds of graves. Early
Canarios used stone coffins, as well
as caves, to bury their dead. Here,
the stones lie in rubble on the hill at
the southern end of the village.

✚ 19J ✉ Municipality of San Bartolomé
de Tirajana: 55km (34 miles) south of Las
Palmas, 10km (6 miles) north of Playa del
Inglés 🍴 Nearest café in Fataga and at
camel park (€) 🚌 18 from Maspalomas

ARTENARA

Dominated by a statue of Christ, this
pleasant town is the highest on the
island (1,219m/4,000ft). Every
window, balcony or turn of the road
offers thrilling views – from its
northern side towards the
pinewoods of Tamadaba (► 154),
and from its southern side across
the valley in which the Roque
Bentaiga (► 148–149) rises in

splendour. The landscape is riddled with caves, some of them in continuous habitation since pre-Spanish times.

The biggest attraction here is the cave church, the Santuario de la Virgen de la Cuevita. The image of the Virgin and Child stands above an altar and pulpit hewn out of solid rock.

✚ 5E ✉ Municipality of Artenara: 49km (30 miles) southwest of Las Palmas, 91km (56 miles) north of Playa del Inglés 🍴 Good restaurants in town (€–€€€) 🚌 220 from Las Palmas ❓ Fiesta of Santa María de la Cuevita, last Sunday in Aug: grand occasion with cycling competition and torchlit processions

AYACATA

This mountain village, which serves as a staging post on the way to the highest point of the island from the coast, has restaurants, souvenir shops and some tremendous views – particularly in early spring, when the entire mountainside is covered in soft, pale clouds of scented almond blossom.

✚ 18G ✉ Municipality of Tejeda: 42km (26 miles) southwest of Las Palmas, 35km (21 miles) north of Playa del Inglés 🚌 18 from Maspalomas/Playa del Inglés

CRUZ DE TEJEDA

At 1,450m (4,756ft), this intricate stone cross, set in a rather scruffy square, full of stands with rather persistent owners, marks the notional centre of the island. The adjacent parador, a white house with exposed stone coigning and green woodwork, which has seen better days, was built as a hotel in 1938 to a traditional design by Néstor Martín Fernández de la Torre. Néstor (1887–1938) studied at the Academy of Fine Art in Madrid but kept his roots alive in the city of his birth, Las Palmas. Many of his canvases – such as *Poema del Atlántico* – depict aspects of the island in a romantic, free-flowing manner. See his work at the Museo Néstor (► 86) in the Pueblo Canario. He also painted the controversial murals in the Teatro Pérez Galdós (► 92), which shocked respectable theatregoers at the time.

There are beautiful views of the surrounding countryside from the side of the parador, which is at present closed for repairs; it is not expected to reopen for visitors to stay in for the forseeable future.

🔹 6E 🖂 Municipality of Tejeda: 37km (33 miles) southwest of Las Palmas 🍴 Food stands and restaurant in area (€–€€) 🚌 305 from Las Palmas; 18 from Maspalomas

EMBALSE DE SORIA

This reservoir, built in 1971 at the head of the Barranco de Arguineguín, is the largest on the island, supplying water to the southern tourist resorts. It is also a popular swimming and fishing lake, fringed with

Canarian palms standing among *taginastes* and *tabaiba*. Walkers who have laboured up the *barranco* often take a welcome break in the small village above the dam and sample the good local dishes.

The only thing that disturbs the general tranquillity is the weekend convoys of jeeps, which climb past Soria to the next reservoir, the Embalse de la Cueva de las Niñas. To the east, the Chira reservoir completes a trio of artificial lakes.

✚ 17H ✉ Municipality of Mogán: 87km (54 miles) south of Las Palmas; 35km (21 miles) northwest of Playa del Inglés 🍴 In village (€)

FATAGA

This town of white houses with pink roofs is praised as an example of all that is loveliest in Canarian villages – not least by its own inhabitants. They describe their home as *tipico, pequeño, bonito* (traditional, small and pretty) and themselves, with no false modesty, as *muy amables* (very kindly).

Fataga's reputation has spread and the village now has several bars and souvenir shops on either side of the main street. This is the thoroughfare connecting San Bartolomé de Tirajana in the centre and Playa del Inglés in the south. But the village itself seems timeless. It falls steeply into curved terraces like stacked plates and ends in a *barranco* floor bristling with palms.

The tiny church, planted around with shady trees, was built in 1880 and bears a plaque marking its centenary and commemorating those who built *tan magna obra* (such a great work).

✚ 19J ✉ San Bartolomé de Tirajana: 60km (37 miles) south of Las Palmas, 16km (10 miles) north of Playa del Inglés 🍴 El Abaricoque (€) and cafés in village (€) 🚌 18 from Maspalomas/Playa del Inglés

FORTALEZA GRANDE

Rising from the valley floor on the west side of highway GC65, to the south of Santa Lucía, this fortress-like rock formation was the scene, in April 1483, of the last resistance of the aboriginal people against their Spanish conquerors. The final nucleus of 600 men and over 1,000 women and children were urged to surrender by their former king, Tenesor Semidan, who had joined the Spanish side and been baptized as a Christian. Refusing to listen, many of his former comrades threw themselves off the cliffs to their deaths.

✚ 20J ✉ Santa Lucía de Tirajana: 42km (26 miles) south of Las Palmas, 28km (17 miles) north of Playa del Inglés 🍴 Cafés at Santa Lucia (€–€€)

ROQUE BENTAIGA

This dramatic monolith, raised like a rugged forearm with clenched fist, surges up to 1,415m (4,642ft) from its own rocky massif, set in a broad valley. Visible from many points in the west and centre of the island, it is accessible by (very winding) road. For the aboriginal inhabitants of the island it was a sacred place and a scene of sacrifices. Bentaiga also made a most effective fortress, playing an important role in the resistance against the Spaniards. Its defenders, under cover of darkness, finally retreated from here to Ansite, where they congregated for their last stand. About 2km (1.2 miles) along the road from the Bentaiga/El Espinillo turning, in the westward extension of the massif, is Cueva del Rey, a large, man-made cave, once painted, with side-chambers and floor holes.

🚩 5E ✉ Municipality of Tejeda: 46km (29 miles) southwest of Las Palmas, 35km (21 miles) north of Playa del Inglés ❓ 30 mins' climb from the parking area on track signed to Bentaiga

ROQUE NUBLO

Roque Nublo stands sentinel over the small town of Tejeda. Though it is a little lower in altitude than the island's highest point at Pozo de las Nieves (1,803m/5,914ft compared to 1,951m/6,401ft), this spectacular basalt monolith dominates many views in the centre of Gran Canaria. It appears to be the final, irreducible core of a far higher volcanic mountain, formed about 3.5 million years ago and long since peeled away by the action of wind, water, snow and ice. One other, smaller rock, El Fraile, stands close to it.

There is a footpath from the car park to the rocky plateau from which Roque Nublo rises, and a footpath right round the little massif makes a spectacular two-hour walking circuit (▶ 150–151).

🚩 6F ✉ Municipality of Tejeda: 48km (30 miles) southwest of Las Palmas, 37km (23 miles) north of Playa del Inglés

a walk around Roque Nublo

This well-kept path makes a complete circuit of Roque Nublo and ascends to the plateau where it stands. It involves gentle descents and one stiffer climb, worth it for wonderful vistas, embracing deep valleys, glimpses of the ocean, the Bentaiga monolith and nearer rocky mountain crests.

Leave the parking area by a small paved area, to follow the ridge directly ahead.

Views of Ayacata open out to the left, and there are fine views from the right-hand side of the ridge.

Near a finger of rock, the path begins to hairpin up; some 75m (80yds) before the rock the path divides. Follow the right-hand path to make the circuit beneath Roque Nublo (left ascends directly to Nublo). The path leads gently down (take care not to slip on pine needles) to the northwestern corner beneath Roque Nublo.

From here, a ridge to the right leads to a castle-like rock outcrop (don't try to climb this), with surprising views of the valley and of Roque Bentaiga (add 20 minutes for the diversion).

Back on the main path, climb gently upwards, then more steeply.

There is a clear view of Roque Nublo – formed in the island's second great wave of volcanic activity – from below, with the lesser rock, El Fraile, now in silhouette.

After 10 minutes, take a clear branch of the path left. Another 15 minutes of climbing brings you to a rocky ridge. Turn left here, with rough steps up to the rock plateau and the base of Roque Nublo. Return to the preliminary ridge and turn left and down, passing the point where the path first divided, and return to the parking area.

Distance 6.5km (4 miles)
Time 2 hours; another 2 hours are added by starting and finishing the walk in Ayacata
Start/end point Parking area 2km (1.2 miles) north of Ayacata, steeply up, right-hand turn in Ayacata
Lunch Take your own supplies

SAN BARTOLOMÉ DE TIRAJANA

An agricultural town on the lip of a crater (the Caldera de Tirajana), San Bartolomé is the administrative centre of the municipality that controls the tourist complexes of San Agustín, Playa del Inglés and Maspalomas. Climb its steep and sober streets, or simply wander in its quiet squares and you will find a world far removed from the parched beaches of the deep south: a pastoral landscape of orchards and cultivated terraces.

San Bartolomé de Tirajana is famous for its local liqueur, *guindilla*, distilled from the *guinda* (sour cherry) and combined with rum and sugar. The town is also well known for its wicker baskets.

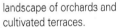 19H ✉ Municipality of San Bartolomé de Tirajana: 52km (32 miles) southwest of Las Palmas, 24km (15 miles) north of Playa del Inglés 🍴 Cafés in town (€–€€€) 🚌 18 from Maspalomas; 34 from Agüimes

SANTA LUCÍA

Visitors come in droves to Santa Lucía's major attraction – its museum, **Museo Castillo de la Fortaleza,** in a former farmhouse now transformed into a pastiche of a turreted castle. It contains an extraordinary jumble of old rocks, guns, stuffed birds, pressed flowers and amazing Guanche or pre-Spanish artefacts. These include pottery, tools, scraps of funerary clothes and other textiles made from reeds, astonishingly well-preserved, and a couple of skeletons. After the museum, visitors usually have lunch in the adjoining rustic-style restaurant, Hao (▶ 157).

Apart from these small diversions, which can create a traffic bottleneck, Santa Lucía is just another attractive mountain village

presided over by its grand neoclassical church of white wall and dark grey stone. The business here is agriculture, particularly fruit-growing; the local liqueur is *mejunje*, made from a mixture of lemons, rum and honey.

✚ 20H ✉ Municipality of Santa Lucía: 45km (30 miles) southwest of Las Palmas, 31km (20 miles) north of Playa del Inglés 🚌 34 from Agüímes or San Bartolomé de Tirajana

Museo Castillo de la Fortaleza

✉ Calle Tomás Arroyo Cardoso ☎ 928 79 80 07 🕐 Daily 9–5 ✋ Inexpensive 🍴 Restaurant in museum (€€)

TAMADABA

Some 8km (5 miles) from Artenara you will
find the island's largest forest of Canary pines,
much loved by walkers and picnickers, centred
on the Pico de Tamadaba at 1,444m (4,736ft).
There is a forestry station on the road round
the mountain and an ICONA (national
environmental agency) picnic site on the edge
of the woods. There are splendid views from
the summit to the coast and, on a clear day,
to Mount Teide on Tenerife.

➕ 4D ✉ Municipality of Agaete: 57km (35 miles)
west of Las Palmas, 99km (61 miles) northwest of
Playa del Inglés

TEJEDA

This peaceful, attractive mountain village is
little visited because most people are en route
to the tourist heart or centre of the island –
the Cruz de Tejeda (➤ 144).

Many young people have left Tejeda to find
work in the tourist-related industries and as a
result the production of sweets and cakes
made from local almonds is now under threat.
In July 2007, a catastrophic fire engulfed the
mountain slopes and the almond orchards
around the village, and locals are waiting to
see how many of the ancient trees will
regenerate spontaneously.

➕ 6E ✉ Municipality of Tejeda: 37km (23 miles)
southwest of Las Palmas, 78km (48 miles) north of
Playa del Inglés 🍴 Bar in village (€) 🚌 305 from
Las Palmas; 18 from Maspalomas

TEMISAS

Temisas is an attractive village half-way up a mountainside, famous for its rural architecture – there are white stone houses with pink tiled roofs, windows with wooden shutters, a little 18th-century whitewashed church with a belfry, a water mill and hillsides dotted with olive trees (Temisas is sometimes known as 'Little Jerusalem').

As in many inland villages, though, depopulation is a problem, with the young leaving for coastal towns in search of almost any work that is easier than tilling terraces.

From the village there are clear views down to a coast of plastic greenhouses, with the town of Arinaga (➤ 106) in the distance. The view is broken by the nearby bulk of a very solid rocky outcrop, unimaginatively named El Roque, rising from the plain beneath.

✚ 20H ✉ Municipality of Agüimes: 35km (22 miles) south of Las Palmas, 33km (20 miles) north of Playa del Inglés
🍴 Bar in village (€) 🚌 34 from Agüimes

HOTELS

SAN BARTOLOMÉ DE TIRAJANA
La Hacienda del Molino (€)
This beautifully restored old *gofio* mill complex on the edge of
town offers 10 traditionally furnished bedrooms set around a
pleasant courtyard where you can take breakfast. The dining room
serves traditional Canarian dishes using local produce.

✉ Calle Los Naranjos 2 ☎ 928 12 73 44; www.lahaciendadelmolino.com

TEJEDA
El Refugio (€€)
A rural hotel with 10 double rooms decorated in Canarian style.
Good base for a walking holiday.

✉ Cruz de Tejeda s/n ☎ 928 66 65 13; www.hotelruralelrefugio.com

RESTAURANTS

TEJEDA
Cueva de la Tea (€€)
A good, unpretentious restaurant in Tejeda, specializing in
roast meat.

✉ C/Dr Hernández Guerra, Tejeda 🕐 Lunch

El Refugio (€€)
In an incomparable situation among the high peaks of the
island, this restaurant in Tejeda is very popular with tour groups.
It offers a varied Canarian menu that is both satisfyingly filling
and delicious.

✉ Cruz de Tejeda ☎ 928 66 65 13; www.hotelruralelrefugio.com
🕐 Lunch

Yolanda (€€)
Next door to El Refugio, with wonderful views from the balcony
(across to Tenerife weather permitting). Excellent hearty mountain
fare of roast meats served with local vegetables, plus some
international dishes.

✉ Cruz de Tejeda, Tejeda ☎ 928 66 62 76 🕐 Daily 9–7

SANTA LUCIA DE TIRAJANA
Hao (€€)
Country food is served at this mountainside village. The restaurant is particularly popular with visitors to the neighbouring Museum of Canarian Life. Arrive before 12:30, or after 2, to avoid coach parties.

✉ C/Tomas Arroyo Cardosa, Santa Lucia de Tirajana ☎ 928 79 80 07
🕐 Lunch

SHOPPING

SAN BARTOLOMÉ DE TIRAJANA
Bar Martin
The agricultural town of San Bartolomé de Tirajana is famous for its local liqueur, *guindilla*, distilled from sour cherries. The liqueur is on sale at this bar.

✉ C/Reyes Catolicos

Bodega Vino Tinto
This attractively laid-out shop, also in San Bartolomé de Tirajana is filled with local produce from the island, with a leaning towards Canarian wines.

✉ C/Reyes Católicos

TEJEDA
Dulcería Nublo
Delicious almond sweets and cakes made from the local almonds are sold in this shop. It is well known for its *mazapan* (almond cake).

✉ C/Dr Hernández Guerraa ☎ 928 66 60 30

ACTIVITIES

WALKING
Walking in the mountains is a popular activity on Gran Canaria, particularly with the younger generation. Older folk remember a time when there were few roads on the island and walking was the only method of transport. Not surprisingly, they prefer to ride

in motorcars. Caminos Reales, literally 'royal ways', are a network of paths once guaranteed by royal authority. They now form the basis of much of the island's walking tracks.

Several hiking groups offer accompanied walks in the more remote parts of the island. These are usually run by foreign residents and are often oversubscribed. If you walk alone, make sure someone knows where you are heading and can raise the alarm if necessary.

The reservoirs of Chira, Soria and Cueva de las Niñas (► 144–145), in the west central part of the island, offer areas to relax beside the water but away from the coast. In some places you can swim off a small beach or dive off rocks. It is possible to hike between all three reservoirs.

NATIVE PLANTS

The central area of the island is a good place to see the wide variety of Gran Canaria's native plants. Common endemic species include the *Pinus canariensis*, or Canary pine, which has the useful talent of regeneration after fire: new growth emerges from seemingly lifeless, charred bark. The hard wood of the tree, called tea, is used for ceilings and balconies. The rock rose *(Cistus symphytifolius)* and asphodel *(Asphodelus microcarpus)* grow in pine forests. The extraordinary-looking dragon tree *(Dracaena draco)*, closely related to the yucca plant, has become the botanical symbol of the Canary Islands. With branches like the legs of a stumpy grey elephant, ending in a spiky green crown, this primitive form of plant is extremely long-lived. Early Guanches dried the red resin of dragon trees, which they used as medicine and as a dye, and islanders still use it as a cure for toothache.

You will notice differences in the flora in different areas, but look out for the huge green and white flower heads of euphorbia, tall spikes of echium and the sweeping, honey-scented fronds of *retama*, Canary Island broom. If you're in the mountains, watch out for spreads of lavender and rosemary; locals set their beehives near patches of these fragrant plants and you'll find the honey for sale at wayside stalls throughout the central area.

The North

Teror

Before the mushroom-like growth of the southern resorts, the cloudier, rainier, greener and far more fertile north of Gran Canaria was the place to be. Both of the island's pre-Hispanic kingdoms had their centres here: one in Gáldar, in the northwest, the other at Telde, in the northeast. The capital of Las Palmas, in the island's northeastern corner, became one of the leading cities of the Spanish nation. Behind Las Palmas, the hills are lushly suburban, but the landscape is surprising, interspersed as it is with volcanic craters and cones.

Inland towns and villages such as Teror, Gáldar and Arucas offer fine old Canarian architecture. Because of the general sense of fertility and greenery, the *barrancos* appear softened, and some – Agaete above all – produce fine tropical and subtropical fruits.

AGAETE

Agaete stands at the mouth of the lush, green *barranco* of the same name. The town of Agaete was founded in 1481; a plaque near the church records the greetings of King Juan Carlos on its 500th anniversary, recalling his visit to 'this pretty corner of Spain'.

The grand church, the Iglesia de la Concepción, sometimes exhibits a fine 16th-century Flemish triptych altarpiece of the *Virgin and Child*, commissioned by a local sugar cane baron from the painter Joos van Cleve (1485–1540). At one time, the central panel of the Virgin was housed in Agaete, and the side panels, showing St Francis of Assisi and St Anthony of Padua, in the chapel in Puerto de las Nieves (▶ 170), the town port. Nowadays, the pieces of the picture have been reunited and the painting spends much of the year at the port, being brought to Agaete for the festival of Bajada de la Rama.

The green and fruitful Barranco de Agaete – producing mangoes and papayas, avocados, figs and coffee – eases the spirit after the harshness of so much of the island's volcanic landscape. There is one substantial tourist development, with privately owned houses and apartments, on the northern side of the valley. Elsewhere, villages run down on spurs from the *barranco* or cling to the steep slopes.

✚ 4C ✉ Municipality of Agaete: 37km (23 miles) west of Las Palmas, 89km (55 miles) north of Playa del Inglés 🚌 103 from Las Palmas ❓ *Bajada de la Rama*, 4 Aug: a Christianized festival with strong aboriginal roots

ARUCAS

Arucas is a lively, populous town with one extraordinary feature –
the needle-pointed, frilly, neo-Gothic Iglesia de San Juan Bautista,
so commanding in size and colour that it is often mistakenly called
a cathedral. Built in a local grey basalt – *piedra azul* (blue stone) –
it was begun in 1909 and completed in 1977. The wide streets are
the legacy of a town planner's efforts in the mid-19th century.

Arucas used to be known as *la villa de las flores* (the town of
flowers), and has fine subtropical gardens in the Municipal Park.
Most of the greenery surrounding the modern town, however, is
that of banana plantations, giving rise to a new description of
Arucas: *republica bananera* (banana republic).

Sugar cane and, even more so, the rum made from it, are also famous local products. An old-established distillery just beneath the town on the north side produces 50,000 litres (11,000 gallons) of rum a day under the label Arehucas – the old Guanche name for the town. The distillery (➤ 73) and the **Museo del Ron** (Rum Museum) are both open to visitors.

Half a kilometre (0.3 miles) further on is the **Jardín de Marquesa.** Developed in the late 19th century, the garden displays 42 types of palm trees, 400 different plants, bushes and trees and is well worth a visit.

To the northeast of town, from the great volcanic cone of Montaña de Arucas – scene of the death of the last great aboriginal freedom fighter, Doramas, in 1481 – there are views of La Isleta and the Bay of Las Palmas.

🚏 8B ✉ Municipality of Arucas: 18km (11 miles) west of Las Palmas, 70km (43 miles) north of Playa del Inglés

🍴 Cafés in town (€–€€)

🚌 205, 206, 210 from Las Palmas ❓ Feast day of St John, 24 Jun

Museo del Ron

✉ Era de San Pedro, 2 ☎ 928 60 00 50 🕐 Mon–Fri 10–2

✋ Free

Jardín de Marquesa

✉ Carretera a Bañderos

☎ 928 31 17 73; www.jardindelamarquesa.com

🕐 Mon–Sat 9–1, 2–6

✋ Moderate

LA ATALAYA

This once entirely troglodytic village 5km (3 miles) west of Santa Brígida (➤ 172–173) now has its fair share of free-standing buildings. But it continues to produce the kind of handmade pottery first made by the aboriginal Canarios, without the use of the wheel and unglazed. It is sold by individual craftspeople from their cave workshops at the edge of the village. La Atalaya and the villages of Iloya de Pineda and Lugarejo are the main centres of pottery handicraft.

✚ 9D ✉ Municipality of Santa Brígida: 12km (7 miles) south of Las Palmas, 52km (32 miles) north of Playa del Inglés 🚌 311 from Las Palmas

LOS BERRAZALES

Set at the upper end of the Barranco de Agaete, Los Berrazales used to be a spa. An old-fashioned spa hotel, Princesa Guayarmina still has guests but their activities are somewhat restricted now that the water is all bottled under the name Cumbres de Gáldar. Los Berrazales marks the start of the trail ascending inland to the high centre of the island and down to the north coast. Once it was busy with donkey traffic, moving grain one way to be milled and ground *gofio* the other. But the reservoirs above now retain all the water and the watermills are in ruins.

✚ 5C ✉ Municipality of Agaete: 42km (26 miles) southwest of Las Palmas, 89km (55 miles) northwest of Playa del Inglés 🍴 Casa Romántica, Valle de Agaete (€€), Hotel Princesa Guayarmina (€€) 🚌 102 from Gáldar

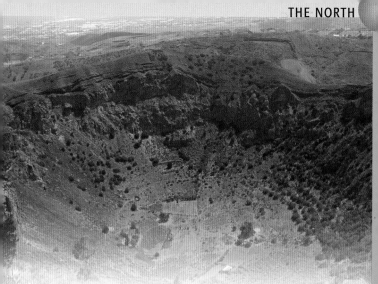

CALDERA DE BANDAMA

The *caldera* (crater) of Bandama forms a perfect bowl, 1km (0.6 miles) across and 200m (656ft) deep, with no way out at the bottom. Its slopes are made up of dark grey ash, but the floor of the crater is patchily fertile, containing a single farm with chickens and goats, figs, oranges, palms and potatoes. The farmer is something of a celebrity. You can walk down into the crater (about 1 hour) from the tiny hamlet of Bandama, taking a path past the church. Take care, though, as the steps soon peter out.

There are superb views from the adjacent Pico de Bandama *mirador* (574m/1,883ft). On the seaward side, there are lofty views over the two Tafiras (➤ 174–175) and to Las Palmas. On the west side is the Club de Golf Bandama, the oldest golf club in Spain.

✚ 10D ✉ Municipality of Santa Brígida: 2km (1.2 miles) south of Tafira Alta, reached via GC110 from Las Palmas 🍽 Club de Golf bar (€€), Las Geranios bar in village (€€), opening times erratic 🚌 311 from Las Palmas

CENOBIO DE VALERÓN

Best places to see, ➤ 42–43.

CUATRO PUERTAS

Cuatro Puertas (Four Doors) was a major religious site, used by the aboriginal people of northeastern Gran Canaria. Four cave openings lead into a single large chamber. An open space in front was presumably ceremonial. The site is close to the summit of a windy hill, Montaña de Cuatro Puertas. From here, you see that the hill is part of the otherwise vanished rim of a volcano.

✠ 22G ✉ Municipality of Telde: 19km (12 miles) south of Las Palmas, 35km (22 miles) northeast of Playa del Inglés ✋ Free 🍴 None on site; bar in village below (€) 🚌 35 from Agüímes or Telde

CUEVAS DE LAS CRUCES

About 5km (3 miles) north of Agaete on the Gáldar road, Cuevas de las Cruces consists of a number of adjoining rock chambers originally inhabited by the Guanches. The corner is awkward – take care entering and especially leaving the parking area.

✠ 5B ✉ Municipality of Gáldar: 34km (21 miles) west of Las Palmas, 86km (53 miles) northwest of Playa del Inglés ✋ Free 🚌 103 from Las Palmas/Gáldar

FIRGAS

Pleasant little upland Firgas, 'capital' of the smallest municipality in Gran Canaria, is famous for its natural spring water: the bottling plant 5km (3 miles) out of town bottles 250,000 litres

(55,000gal) a day. Firgas is also an agricultural community.

✠ 7C ✉ Municipality of Firgas: 25km (15.5 miles) west of Las Palmas, 78km (48 miles) north of Playa del Inglés 🚌 201, 202 from Las Palmas; 211 from Arucas

GÁLDAR

The most historic of all Guanche towns and now the centre of a banana-growing area, Gáldar shelters from the sea behind the volcanic cone of Montaña de Gáldar. It has an excellent covered market in the main street and a fine square, Plaza de Santiago. The church, with its wide neoclassical facade, unusually built in a pale fawn-coloured stone, stands on the site of the palace of the former Guanche kings. There is also a monument to Tenesor Semidan, the last king of Gáldar, on Calle Guariragua, unveiled by King Juan Carlos I of Spain in 1986. The town hall is a building of real charm in the best Canarian-Hispanic style.

Below the town you can visit the **museum and archaeological park** of the famous Guanche **Cueva Pintada** (Painted Cave), discovered by chance in 1873. This unique site and its interpretation centre will fill you in on the ancient Guanche people, their customs and their way of life. The tour starts with a 3D film and includes a visit to the Painted Cave itself, decorated with squares, circles and triangles etched on the cave walls in red, black and white, as well as the museum and its finds.

✚ 5B ✉ Municipality of Gáldar: 27km (17 miles) west of Las Palmas, 79km (49 miles) northwest of Playa del Inglés 🍴 Bar in market (€), cafés on Calle Capitán Guesada 🚌 103, 105 from Las Palmas

Museo y Parque Arqueológico Cueva Pintada

☎ 928 89 57 46 (pre-booking essential) 🕐 Tue–Sat 9:30–8 (last tour 6:30) ✋ Moderate

LA GUANCHA

On an arid site, hemmed in by houses and banana plantations, substantial remains of pre-Hispanic dwelling places and communal tombs survive. In the larger tombs, a central shaft is surrounded

by two rows of radial chambers, all of it encircled by a final wall –
like chapels lining the apse in a Christian cathedral. Forty-three
people were buried in the largest.

🚩 5A ✉ Municipality of Gáldar: 29km (18 miles) west of Las Palmas, 81km
(50 miles) northwest of Playa del Inglés 🖐 Free 🍴 Bar in El Agujero (€)

JARDÍN BOTÁNICO CANARIA
Best places to see, ➤ 46–47.

MOYA
Seen from the west Moya is an astonishing place, with a huge
church, Nuestra Señora de la Candelaria, perched on the very
lip of a deep ravine. Moya includes the birthplace of the poet
and doctor Tomás Morales (1885–1921), now the **Casa Museo
Tomás Morales.** Moya was home town of the Guanche leader
Doramas. He moved to Telde when he became *guanarteme* (king),
only to die resisting Spanish conquest in 1481.

🚩 7B ✉ Municipality of Moya: 31km (19 miles) west of Las Palmas,
90km (56 miles) north of Playa del Inglés 🍴 Cafés in town (€–€€€) 🚌 116,
117 from Las Palmas; 123 from Arucas

Casa Museo Tomás Morales
✉ Plaza de Tomás Morales 1 ☎ 928 62 02 17 🕐 Mon–Fri 9–8, Sat 10–8,
Sun 10–2 🖐 Free

PUERTO DE LAS NIEVES

Puerto de las Nieves is the home port of Agaete, capital in turn of a rich agricultural area. For centuries, this was the only reasonable point of access to this part of the island. A ferry service from Tenerife carries day-trippers and their rental cars in both directions. One dark grey beach huddles under the cliff, looking south at the Dedo de Dios (Finger of God), a slender monolith left standing when the rest of the cliff was eroded; the top part was broken off during a tropical storm in 2005. Next comes the harbour and a promenade, the Paseo de las Poetas.

🚩 4C ✉ Municipality of Agaete: 39km (24 miles) west of Las Palmas, 91km (56 miles) northwest of Playa del Inglés 🍴 Fish restaurants on Paseo de las Poetas (€–€€€) 🚌 103 from Las Palmas ⛴ Daily ferries to Tenerife (six ferries a day, 1-hour journey; www.fredolsen.es)

REPTILANDIA

Set on the dusty slopes of an extinct volcano (Montaña Almagro), this park breeds and displays reptiles and amphibians. Snakes from all over the world, many of them deadly, are housed in glass cases, all identified by scientific and common name (in English and in German) and place of origin. In addition to the three indoor exhibition rooms, there are large outdoor terrariums of crocodiles, alligators, turtles, tortoises, lizards and frogs. These have been designed – with waist-high walls and a roof net – to allow the animals maximum protection in a natural-looking habitat that is also easily accessible to spectators. The owner is British zoologist Jim Pether.

Don't miss the star attraction, the world's largest lizard, the Komodo dragon.

✚ 4B ✉ Ctra Norte, km 24, Gáldar: 31km (19 miles) west of Las Palmas. From the south take GC1 to link with GC2 at Las Palmas, go on to Agaete, then follow signs from Hoya de Pineda exit ☎ 928 55 12 69 🕒 Daily 11–5:30 ✋ Moderate 🍴 Snacks on premises (€) 🚌 102 to Cruz de Pineda, then follow signs for Reptilandia (1km/0.6 miles)

SANTA BRÍGIDA

This comfortable, affluent town is so well connected by fast road
to Las Palmas, that it is now virtually a suburb of the capital city.
Despite whitewashed houses and Canarian balconies, Santa
Brígida has less of a Spanish feel to it than any other town on the
island. Its wide, tree-lined streets and large villas set in spacious
gardens owe much to early British settlers, many of them involved
in the wine, and then the banana, business. Though often working
in Las Palmas, they made their homes here, attracted by the
town's altitude and cooler temperatures. Santa Brígida and its
neighbourhood are noted for their excellent restaurants
(► 182–183).

✠ 9D ✉ Municipality of Santa Brígida: 15km (9 miles) southwest of Las Palmas, 55km (34 miles) north of Playa del Inglés 🍴 Many cafés (€–€€€) 🚌 301, 302, 303, 305 from Las Palmas

SANTA MARÍA DE GUÍA

Usually known simply as Guía, this town lies 3km (2 miles) east of its neighbour, Gáldar. As in Gáldar, it pays to leave the main road and enter the old quarter, climbing briefly if steeply up narrow but stately streets (start where the road makes an awkward bend).

Among the early settlers of Guía were Genoese bankers and merchants, so the town has some fine architecture, such as the 16th-century Casa Quintana. The centrepiece is an old-fashioned main square with trees and a church (Santa María) in stern volcanic grey and white – in this case, however, with a floridly neo-classical façade designed by José Luján Pérez, Canarian sculptor–architect and native son of Guía. Begun in 1607, the interior of the church mixes baroque with neoclassical. The elegant town hall, in Canarian style, is also in the square.

Guía is well known for craft – basketwork, carved-handled knives – but its most famous product is *queso de flor* (flower-cheese), made of goat's milk flavoured with artichoke flowers, best bought in the establishment belonging to Sr Santiago Giol, at Calle Marqués del Muni 34.

✠ 6B ✉ Municipality of Santa María de Guía: 24km (15 miles) west of Las Palmas, 76km (47 miles) northwest of Playa del Inglés 🍴 Cafés in town (€–€€€) 🚌 103, 105 from Las Palmas

SARDINA

This is a little town of modern appearance right in the northwestern corner of the island. It faces south with views over the white-crested sea and along the magnificent coastline. Among the town's attractions are some cave dwellings, cave boathouses and, as often, a cave restaurant. Called, simply, La Cueva (➤ 183), it is tucked in where the road rounds the small grey sand beach.

🚼 4A ✉ Municipality of Gáldar: 33km (20 miles) west of Las Palmas, 85km (53 miles) northwest of Playa del Inglés 🍴 Cafés in town (€–€€€) 🚌 103, 105 from Las Palmas to Gáldar, then taxi to Sardina

TAFIRA ALTA Y BAJA

The towns of Tafira Alta and Baja are now no more than comfortable residential suburbs of Las Palmas. Like Santa Brígida, the area is known for good food. The nearby Jardín Canario has an excellent restaurant and superb views by its top entrance. At the lower level, you can eat well in the village of La Calzada. The name of caves in the nearby *barranco*,

Cuevas de los Frailes, recalls evangelizing friars who were murdered by resistant Guanches. These same friars are immortalized in the name of a hotel, Los Frailes, built by an Englishman at the end of the 19th century, now a private house on the road above the Jardín Canario. Nearby Monte Lentiscal and Monte Coello are regarded as the best wine-producing areas in the island.

✚ Alta 9D; Baja 10C ✉ Municipality of Las Palmas: 8km (5 miles) south of Las Palmas, 53km (33 miles) northeast of Playa del Inglés 🍴 Cafés in both towns (€–€€€) 🚌 301, 302 from Las Palmas

TELDE

Telde, in the east of the island and south of Las Palmas, is Gran Canaria's second largest town. Historically, it was the seat of the *guanarteme* (king), who controlled the eastern part of the island. Its environs are not inviting. The modern town centre is busy and thrumming with traffic. The old town centre is the best bit.

The most picturesque part is the *barrio* of San Francisco – a place of stone-coigned white houses, wooden balconies and pitched roofs around the 18th-century Church of San Francisco, home to rich merchants in earlier days. The major church, though, is San Juan Bautista (St John the Baptist), surrounded by cobbled streets and a pleasant square in the north of the town. It was begun early in the 16th century. Inside, above the ornate gilt *retablo*, is a life-size figure of Christ sculpted from crushed maize, and weighing only some 5kg (11 pounds). It was made by Mexican Indians and indicates the amount of two-way traffic between the New World and the Canary Islands.

The **Casa Museo León y Castillo** is the former home of Juan de León y Castillo, the engineer who built the harbour at Las Palmas.

🚰 11E ✉ Municipality of Telde: 21km (13 miles) south of Las Palmas, 77km (48 miles) northeast of Playa del Inglés 🚌 12 from Las Palmas; 36, 90 from Maspalomas

Casa Museo León y Castillo

✉ Calle León y Castillo 43–45 ☎ 928 69 13 77 🕐 Mon–Fri 9–8, Sat–Sun 10–1 ♿ Free 🍴 Near museum (€–€€)

TEROR

Best places to see, ➤ 52–53.

LOS TILOS

The name refers to the surviving one per cent of Gran Canaria's original and ancient *laurasilva* (laurel) forest, now under rigorous protection. You may survey it from the very narrow road that runs through it but you are not allowed to wander in it.

➕ 7C ✉ Municipality of Moya: 34km (21 miles) southwest of Las Palmas, 87km (54 miles) north of Playa del Inglés 🍴 Los Tilos (€€€) ❓ On minor road off Moya–Guía road, 3km (2 miles) from Moya

VEGA DE SAN MATEO

Vega means 'fertile plain', and this prosperous town, known as San Mateo, certainly deserves that description – except in its hilliness. Almond, chestnut and fig trees cover these foothills of the Tejeda crater, and terraced plots produce the best pears and peaches on the island.

A livestock market is held at first light on Sunday mornings. The general market takes place in two huge hangars on the south side of town, one offering all the abundance of the land while the second items such as cassettes and felt slippers. In between the two, traders lay their pottery and basketwork out on the ground.

La Cantonera is a privately owned museum of rural life, together with a 15-room hotel and a restaurant (➤ 61).

➕ 8E ✉ Municipality of Vega de San Mateo: 21km (13 miles) southwest of Las Palmas, 61km (38 miles) north of Playa del Inglés 🚌 303 from Las Palmas ❓ Town fiesta, Romería de San Mateo, 21 Sep

La Cantonera
✉ Avenida de Tinamar 17
☎ 928 66 17 95 🕐 Daily 10–3
✋ Moderate 🍴 Restaurant (€€)
Mon–Sat 1–4, 9–midnight,
Sun 1–4

HOTELS

AGAETE
Hotel Princesa Guayarmina (€€)
An old-fashioned spa hotel in a green and fertile valley. Ideal for quiet walks.
✉ Los Berrazales, Valle de Agaete ☎ 928 89 80 09

Las Longueras (€€–€€€)
In a beautiful situation, this 19th-century mansion has been renovated into a country hotel.
✉ Calle Doctor Chil 20, Valle de Agaete km 4 ☎ 928 31 84 00;
www.laslongueras.com

ARUCAS
La Hacienda del Buen Suceso (€€€)
High-quality rural hotel overlooking banana plantations with views to the sea. Pool, jacuzzi and fitness room.
✉ Carretera de Arucas a Bañaderos, km 1 ☎ 928 62 29 45;
www.haciendabuensuceso.com

BANDAMA
Hotel Golf de Bandama (€€€)
A small country house/golf hotel on the edge of the Bandama crater, just 15m (16yds) from the first hole. Most rooms have views of the course and the pool.
✉ Bandama s/n ☎ 928 35 15 38; www.bandamagolf.com

PUERTO DE LAS NIEVES
Hotel Puerto de las Nieves (€€€)
Luxury hotel with many facilities including sauna, jacuzzi and therapy treatments. Close to beach.
✉ Avenida Alcade José Armas ☎ 928 88 62 56;
www.hotelpuertodelasnieves.net

SANTA BRÍGIDA
Hotel Escuela (€€)
In the cool hills of Monte Lentiscal, this hotel is a training school as well as a fully functioning hotel with a splendid dining room, gardens and pool; it enjoys an excellent reputation.

✉ Calle Real de Coello 2 ☎ 928 35 55 11; www.hecansa.org

VEGA DE SAN MATEO
Hotel Rural el Pinar (€€€)
Nine beautifully furnished, rustic rooms. Off the road between Valsequillo and San Mateo, this is an ideal place to walk or relax by the pool. Evening meal by request.

✉ La Parada 26 (Tenteniguada), Valsequillo ☎ 928 70 52 39

RESTAURANTS

AGAETE
Casa Pepe (€€)
A cheerful, popular place to eat meat or fish. Good value.

✉ Calle Alcalde Armas Galván 5 ☎ 928 89 82 27 🕑 Thu–Tue lunch, dinner

Casa Romántica (€€)
A delightful restaurant which serves both international and Spanish food using fresh produce.

✉ Valle de Agaete, km 3.5 ☎ 928 89 80 84 🕑 Lunch only

Princesa Guayarmina (€€€)
The restaurant of a former spa hotel, a little run-down but sweetly old-fashioned and surrounded by splendid scenery, serves Canarian food.

✉ Valle de Agaete, km 7 ☎ 928 89 80 09 🕑 Lunch, dinner

ARUCAS
Casa Brito (€-€€)
This smart restaurant with rustic decoration opened in 1998. Good choice of Canarian and Argentinian dishes, including *morcilla canaria* (Canarian black pudding). Small wine list.

✉ Pasaje de Ter 17 ☎ 928 62 23 23 🕑 Wed–Sun lunch, dinner

La Barca (€€)

Much praised fish and seafood restaurant in San Andrés, a fishing hamlet in the municipality of Arucas. Your choice depends on the day's catch.

✉ Carretera del Norte 26, San Andrés ☎ 928 62 60 88 🕐 Tue–Sun lunch, dinner

LA ATALAYA
El Castillete (€€)

Select and cook your own meat at the barbecue or on a hot stone at your table. Very popular restaurant, so reserve ahead at weekends.

✉ El Raso 7, La Atalya ☎ 928 35 24 43 🕐 Closed dinner Sun and Mon

FIRGAS
Asaderos Las Brasas (€)

Well known for its chickens, roasted in charcoal grills, this is a typical informal country restaurant, popular with locals as well as tourists. Good value.

✉ Avenida de La Cruz 36 ☎ 928 62 52 50 🕐 Lunch, dinner; closed Tue

GÁLDAR
Alcori Restaurante (€€)

This is a cheerful and bustling restaurant in the centre of the town.

✉ Calle Capitán Quesada ☎ 928 88 36 74 🕐 Lunch, dinner

PUERTO DE LAS NIEVES
Capita (€€)

Freshest fish is on offer in this friendly, bustling, cheerful restaurant.

✉ Puerto de las Nieves 37 ☎ 928 55 41 42 🕐 Lunch, dinner

El Dedo de Dios (€€€)

Seafood soup and fish stew with *gofio* is the speciality here – Canarian fish cooking at its best.

✉ Puerto de las Nieves ☎ 928 89 80 00 🕐 Lunch, dinner

El Puerto de Laguete (€€)

Crowded at weekends and never empty during the week, this fish restaurant is famous for its good food and its warm welcome.

✉ Nuestra Señora de las Nieves 9 ☎ 928 55 40 01 🕐 Tue–Sun lunch, dinner

Faneque (€€€)

This smart restaurant in the Hotel Puerto de las Nieves offers quality international and Canarian dishes, using both meat and fish.

✉ Avenida Alcalde José Armas ☎ 928 88 62 56 🕐 Tue–Sun lunch, dinner

Las Nasas (€€€)

A superb fish restaurant in an area renowned for fish eateries. Terrace to the beach.

✉ Calle Puerto de las Nieves ☎ 928 89 86 50 🕐 Lunch, dinner

SANTA BRÍGIDA

Bentayga (€€)

First-class restaurant using the best of local produce in local cuisine. The meat dishes – try lamb or goat – are recommended.

✉ Carretera del Centro 130, Monte Coello ☎ 928 35 51 86 🕐 Lunch, dinner

Casa Martel (€€€)

This old-fashioned country restaurant has an excellent wine cellar.

✉ Carretera del Centro, km 18, El Madroñal ☎ 928 64 24 83 🕐 Lunch, dinner

Grutas de Artiles (€€€)

Restaurant with a reputation for good Spanish food in a lively setting. Garden, tennis courts, swimming pool and caves.

✉ Las Meleguiñas, Santa Brígida ☎ 928 64 05 75; www.lasgrutasdeartiles.com 🕐 Noon–12:30am

Satautey (€€)

This restaurant in the Hotel Escuela (a working hotel and a hotel training school) wins enthusiastic plaudits for the quality of food and service – a testimony to the professionalism of the catering students in charge.

✉ Calle Real de Coello 2, Santa Brígida ☎ 928 01 04 21 🕐 Lunch, dinner

SARDINA
La Cueva (€€)
A small cave restaurant serving fresh fish, either in the cave or on the terrace outside. Simple but sweet.

✉ Playa de Sardina ☎ 928 88 02 36 🕐 Lunch, dinner

TAFIRA
El Rincón de Betty (€€)
Well off the tourist trail, this restaurant caters for discerning locals who come here to enjoy the best of local cooking in pleasant surroundings. Much of the menu is inspired by traditional mountain food, with a modern twist. There's a good wine list and attentive service.

✉ Carretera de Reventón, El Monte, Tafira ☎ 928 43 05 95 🕐 Lunch, dinner

Jardín Canario (€€€)
A wonderful setting on the edge of the cliff above the botanical gardens. The food is excellent Canarian, the service is elegant.

✉ Carretera del Centro, km 7.200, Tafira Alta ☎ 928 43 09 39 🕐 Lunch, dinner

La Masia de Canarias (€€€)
Country restaurant serving wholesome Canarian food from fresh local ingredients.

✉ Calle Murillo 36, Tafira Alta ☎ 928 35 01 20 🕐 Lunch, dinner

TELDE
La Pardilla (€€)
Northeast of Telde, this restaurant is highly praised for its Canarian cuisine, particularly its *mojo* sauces to accompany charcoal-grilled meat. The *puchero canario*, a rich stew, is another favourite.

✉ Calle Raimundo Lulio 54, La Pardilla ☎ 928 69 51 02 🕐 Tue–Sun lunch, dinner

TEROR
Balcón de la Zamora (€€)
Fine views from the look-out point and excellent kid stew in this
busy restaurant.

✉ Carretera a Valleseco km 8 ☎ 928 61 80 42 ⏰ Lunch, dinner

VEGA DE SAN MATEO
La Cantonera (€€)
Good country cooking in an old farmhouse which is now a
museum of rural life and an excellent hotel in lovely surroundings.

✉ Avenida Tinamar ☎ 928 66 17 95 ⏰ Mon–Sat lunch

La Veguetilla (€€€)
This is an ideal restaurant in which to enjoy a long, slow Sunday
lunch. Traditional Canarian and Spanish food.

✉ Carretera del Centro km 20.300 ☎ 928 66 07 64 ⏰ Wed–Mon lunch,
dinner

SHOPPING

ARUCAS
Destilerías Arehucas
See page 73.

Feluco
Small sculptures and objects made of grey basalt stone, *piedra
azul*, from local quarries. Picture frames, flowers and a model of
the church of San Juan Bautista in Arucas are all sold here.

✉ Calle Dr Fleming ☎ 928 60 54 45

Saturday market
Arucas' busy weekly market, held, as in all major towns, in addition
to the permanent municipal market. If you are in town on
Saturdays, it's worth a stroll round.

✉ Plaza de la Constitución

Roberto Ramirez
See page 73.

LA ATALAYA
Centro Locero
This village has long been a centre of pottery production. There is a strong sense of preserving traditional techniques and the ALUD (Association of Professionals of La Loza of La Atalaya) has a programme of continued research and teaching, as well as organizing the exhibition and sale of items of pottery. Through its work the association is passing knowledge on to a new generation.

✉ Camino de la Picota 11 ☎ 928 28 82 70

GÁLDAR
Tabaiba
This shop sells all sorts of traditional handicrafts and locally made goods.

✉ Capitán Quesada 22 ☎ 928 88 32 82

MOYA
Doramas
See page 76.

SANTA BRÍGIDA
Saturday and Sunday market
A lively small market is held in the open air near the town's parking area. You will find lots of local fruit, vegetables and flowers displayed on the stands, as well as an interesting selection of cheeses, cakes and honey.

✉ Calle Dieciocho

SANTA MARIA DE GUÍA
Juan José Caballero Rodriguez
Juan José Caballero works in wood – traditional country tools and objects, bowls, spoons, boxes and stools. He also sells antiques – and virtually anything else, as long as it is fashioned out of wood.

✉ Calle Lepanto 9 ☎ 928 88 27 79

Los Quesos

A cheese emporium, assorted produce of sheep and goat's milk plus honey, local wine, rum and a good variety of craftwork.

✉ Carretera General Lomo de Guillén

Santiago Gil Romero/El Camino de Gilmani S.L.

Buy *queso de flor de Guía*, a creamy cheese flavoured with artichoke flowers. Cheese in this fascinating relic of a shop is left to mature on bamboo mats.

✉ Calle Marqués de Muni 34 ☎ 928 88 18 75

TAFIRA
La Calzada

On the right-hand side of the road leading to the Jardín Botánico Canario at Tafira Baja, this artisan shop sells a variety of goods made in Gran Canaria.

✉ Tafira Baja ☎ No phone

TEROR
Sunday market

A fascinating selection of local produce, including marzipan cakes from the nearby convent, and Teror's own sausage, *chorizo rojo*.

✉ Plaza del Pino

VEGA DE SAN MATEO
Sunday market

Situated in the centre of a richly agricultural community, this market attracts customers from all over the island.

✉ Avenida del Mercado

ENTERTAINMENT

Club de Golf

Splendid location on the edge of the Bandama crater, near Santa Brígida: 18 holes, par 71, 5,679m (6,190yds) course. Hotel and restaurant attached. Visitors, as temporary members, may play, except at weekends.

✉ Carretera de Bandama s/n ☎ 928 35 01 04 🚌 39

Sight Locator Index

This index relates to the maps on the covers. We have given map references to the main sights of interest in the book. Grid references in italics indicate sights featured on the town plans. Some sights within towns may not be plotted on the maps.

Index

Acknowledgements

The Automobile Association would like to thank the following photographers, companies and picture libraries for their assistance in the preparation of this book.

Abbreviations for the picture credits are as follows: (t) top; (b) bottom; (c) centre; (l) left; (r) right; (AA) AA World Travel Library

4l Fataga, AA/C Sawyer; **4c** Driving in Gran Canaria. AA/C Sawyer; **4r** Teror, AA/C Sawyer; **5l** Statues, Las Palma, AA/P Bennett; **5c** Aguimes, AA/J A Tims; **6/7** Fataga, AA/C Sawyer; **8/9** Telde, AA/C Sawyer; **10/11** Artenara view, AA/J A Tims; **10l** Spanish Galleon, Puerto Rico, AA/J A Tims; **10r** House, Tarifa Alta, AA/J A Tims; **11** Galdar, AA/J A Tims; **12** local cheeses, AA/P Bennett; **13t** Paella, AA/P Bennett; **13c** Arrugadas, AA/P Bennett; **13b** Arucas Rum, AA/P Bennett; **14t** Banana plantation, AA/P Bennett; **14c** Tropical Beer, AA/P Bennett; **14b** Fruit Juice, AA/P Bennett; **14/15t** Freshly caught fish, AA/C Sawyer; **14/15b** Ham, AA/P Bennett; **16** Locals playing dominoes, AA/P Bennett; **16/17** Cuatro Puertas, AA/J A Tims; **18** Jardin Botanico Canario, AA/J A Tims; **19t** Canarian Wrestling, AA/P Bennett; **19b** Folk Group, AA/P Bennett; **20/21** Driving in Gran Canaria. AA/C Sawyer; **25** Woman with flowers, AA/C Sawyer; **27** Ferry AA/P Bennett; **29** Mountain Road, AA/J A Tims; **34/35** Teror, AA/C Sawyer; **36/37** Anden Verde, AA/J A Tims; **38** Local, Barranco de Guayadeque, AA/C Sawyer; **38/39** Cave houses, AA/P Bennett; **39** Cave house, AA/P Bennett; **40** Casa de Colon, AA/J A Tims; **40/41** Interior, Casa de Colon, AA/P Bennett; **41** Log book, AA/P Bennett; **42** Cenobio de Valeron, AA/P Bennett; **42/43** Cenobio de Valeron. AA/P Bennett; **44/45** Dunas de Maspalomas, AA/J A Tims; **46/47** Jardin Botanico Canario, AA/J A Tims; **47** Jardin Botanico Canario, AA/P Bennett; **48** Beach umbrellas, AA/J A Tims; **49** Las Canteras, AA/P Bennett; **50** Restaurants, Puerto Mogan, AA/P Bennett; **50/51** Puerto Mogan, AA/P Bennett; **52** Nuestra Senora del Pino, AA/C Sawyer; **52/53** Teror, AA/P Bennett; **54** Plaza de Santa Ana, AA/C Sawyer; **55** La Vegueta, AA/C Sawyer; **56/57** Statues, Las Palma, AA/P Bennett; **58** Dining Table, AA/C Sawyer; **60/61** Puerto Mogan, AA/C Sawyer; **63** Aqua Sur, AA/J A Tims; **64/65** Golfers, AA/C Sawyer; **66/67** Plaza Cairasco, AA/P Bennett; **68/69** Mundo Aborigien, AA/J A Tims; **71** Puerto Rico, AA/J A Tims; **72/73** Ignenio, souvenirs, AA/J A Tims; **74** Folk dancers, AA/P Bennett; **77** Shopping bags, AA/C Sawyer; **78/79** Aguimes, AA/J A Tims; **81** Santa Ana Cathedral. AA/P Bennett; **83** Las Palmas, AA/P Bennett; **84** Fertility object, AA/P Bennett; **84/85** Museo Elder, AA/P Bennett; **86** Guanche pole-vaulter, AA/P Bennett; **87** Parque Santa Catalina, AA/P Bennett; **88** Parque San Telmo, AA/P Bennett; **90** Las Canteras, AA/P Bennett; **91** Las Palmas, AA/J A Tims; **92t** Folk Dancers, AA/P Bennett; **92b** Teatro Perez Galdos, AA/C Sawyer; **103** San Nicolas de Tolentino, AA/J A Tims; **104** Aguimes, AA/J A Tims; **105** Arguineguin, AA/J A Tims; **106/107** Arigna, AA/J A Tims; **107** Museo de Piedras e Artesainia, AA/J A Tims; **108** Puerto de las Nieves, AA/C Sawyer; **108/109** Agaete, AA/C Sawyer; **110/111** Juan Grande, AA/J A Tims; **112** Maspalomas lagoon, AA/P Bennett; **113** Aqua Sur, AA/J A Tims; **114** Holiday World, AA/J A Tims; **114/115** Camel rides, AA/P Bennett; **115** Mogan, AA/J A Tims; **116** Mundo Aborigen, AA/J A Tims; **116/117** Palmitos Parque, AA/J A Tims; **118** Pasito Blanco, AA/J A Tims; **120/121** Playa del Ingles, AA/P Bennett; **122** Playa del Ingles,. AA/P Bennett; **123** Playa del Ingles, AA/P Bennett; **124/125** Puerto de la Aldea, AA/J A Tims; **126** Puerto Rico, AA/J A Tims; **126/127** Puerto Rico, AA/P Bennett; **128/129** San Augustin, AA/J A Tims; **129** San Nicolas de Tolentino, AA/J A Tims; **130** Vecindario, AA/J A Tims; **141** Embalse de Soria, AA/J A Tims; **142/143** Artenara, AA/J A Tims; **143** Artenara, AA/J A Tims; **144** Cruz de Tejeda, AA/P Bennett; **144/145** Embalse de Soria, AA/J A Tims; **146/147** Tejeda, AA/C Sawyer; **147** Fortaleza Grande, AA/J A Tims; **148** Roque Bentaiga, AA/C Sawyer; **149** Roque Nublo, AA/C Sawyer; **150** Roque Nublo, AA/P Bennett; **151** Tejeda, AA/J A Tims; **152** San Bartolome de Tirajana, AA/P Bennett; **152/153** Castillo de la Forteleza, AA/ J A Tims; **153** Castillo de la Forteleza, AA/J A Tims; **144/145** Tejeda, AA/J A Tims; **155** Temisas, AA/J A Tims; **159** Los Tilos, AA/J A Tims; **160** Barranco de Agaete, AA/C Sawyer; **161** Agaete, AA/P Bennett; **162/163** Arucas, AA/C Sawyer; **163** Arucas Cathedral, AA/P Bennett; **164** Los Berrazales, AA/J A Tims; **165** Caldera de Bandama, AA/J A Tims; **166** Cuatro Puertas, AA/J A Tims; **167** Firgas, AA/P Bennett; **168** Church of Santiago de los Caballeros, AA/J A Tims; **169** Moya, AA/J A Tims; **170/171** Puerto de las Nieves, AA/P Bennett; **171** Reptilandia Park, AA/J A Tims; **172/173** Santa Brigida, AA/J A Tims; **173** Cheeses, AA/J A Tims; **174** Cave house, AA/P Bennett; **174/175** Tafira Baja, AA/J A Tims; **176/177** Telde, AA/C Sawyer; **178** Vega de San Mateo, AA/J A Tims

Every effort has been made to trace the copyright holders, and we apologise in advance for any accidental errors. We would be happy to apply the corrections in the following edition of this publication.

Dear Reader

Your comments, opinions and recommendations are very important to us. Please help us to improve our travel guides by taking a few minutes to complete this simple questionnaire.

You do not need a stamp (unless posted outside the UK). If you do not want to cut this page from your guide, then photocopy it or write your answers on a plain sheet of paper.

Send to: **The Editor, AA World Travel Guides,**
FREEPOST SCE 4598, Basingstoke RG21 4GY.

Your recommendations...

We always encourage readers' recommendations for restaurants, nightlife or shopping – if your recommendation is used in the next edition of the guide, we will send you a **FREE AA Guide** of your choice from this series. Please state below the establishment name, location and your reasons for recommending it.

_____

_____

_____

_____

_____

Please send me **AA Guide** _____

About this guide...

Which title did you buy?

AA _____

Where did you buy it? _____

When? **m m** / **y y**

Why did you choose this guide? _____

_____

_____

_____

Did this guide meet your expectations?

Exceeded ☐ Met all ☐ Met most ☐ Fell below ☐

Were there any aspects of this guide that you particularly liked? _____

_____

_____

_____

continued on next page...

Is there anything we could have done better? _____

_____

_____

About you...
Name (Mr/Mrs/Ms) _____

Address _____

_____

_____ Postcode

Daytime tel nos _____

Email _____

Please only give us your mobile phone number or email if you wish to hear from us about other products and services from the AA and partners by text or mms, or email.

Which age group are you in?
Under 25 ☐ 25–34 ☐ 35–44 ☐ 45–54 ☐ 55–64 ☐ 65+ ☐

How many trips do you make a year?
Less than one ☐ One ☐ Two ☐ Three or more ☐

Are you an AA member? Yes ☐ No ☐

About your trip...
When did you book? m m / y y   When

How long did you stay? _____

Was it for business or leisure? _____

Did you buy any other travel guides for your tri

If yes, which ones? _____

_____

_____

Thank you for taking the time to complete this
possible, and remember, you do not need a sta

AA Travel Insurance call 0800 07